English Victorian Jewellery

Other Books by Ernle Bradford

Contemporary Jewellery and Silver Design
Four Centuries of European Jewellery

Diamond-and-amethyst necklace with scroll-work design that once belonged to Queen Alexandra.
The pendant cross in the centre is in filigree gold with diamonds and pink topaz. (By courtesy of Wartski Ltd)

ENGLISH VICTORIAN JEWELLERY

Ernle Bradford

Spring Books

For Marie Blanche

First published 1959 by Country Life Ltd
© Copyright Ernle Bradford 1959
This edition published 1967 by Spring Books
Hamlyn House · The Centre · Feltham · Middlesex

Printed in Great Britain by Fletcher & Son Ltd, Norwich
and bound by Richard Clay (The Chaucer Press) Ltd, Bungay, Suffolk

Contents

Preface 11

1. The Eighteenth-century Background 13

2. Early Victorian and High Victorian Styles 21

3. Gold Filigree Jewellery and the Etruscan Style 41

4. Semi-precious Jewellery of the Nineteenth Century 53

5. Popular Jewellery: its Ancestry and its Development in the Nineteenth Century 66

6. Techniques and Materials 93

7. The End of an Epoch 108

Conclusion 120

Glossary 124

Selected Bibliography 133

Index 135

5

ACKNOWLEDGMENTS

Thanks are due to the following for the loan of examples of Victorian jewellery for illustration in these pages:

Asprey & Co.
Biggs of Farnham
Cameo Corner
Carrington & Co.
Garrard & Co.
Richard Ogden
The Victoria and Albert Museum
Wartski & Co.

Also to Mr Peter Parkinson, who was responsible for most of the photography.

Illustrations

A representative group of minor 19th-century pieces *page* 17

A tiara in gold, set with diamonds and pearls 18

A brooch in gold and silver, set with rubies, emeralds and diamonds 18

An aigrette in gold set with diamonds and turquoise 18

A brooch in gold set with diamonds and turquoise 18

Seven silver sprays set with diamonds and a gold diamond-set brooch 23

Necklace and ear-rings *en suite*, of silver and gold set with diamonds and sapphires 24

Gold floral brooch set with diamonds, rubies, and emeralds 24

A star cluster brooch of diamonds set in silver 24

Diamond open-work necklace with two floral sprays 33

Early Victorian diamond and ruby brooch with emerald centre 34

Early Victorian open-work scroll brooch 34

A gold brooch set with large amethysts 34

Delicate gold filigree work in a butterfly brooch set with opals and other gemstones 34

Pavé and collet-set rose and brilliant diamonds form a classic formal spray 39

Floral sprays, a briolette and a diamond crescent 39

A large mixed-cut cairngorm surrounded by pearls and garnets 39

The rising-sun motif 39

Carbuncles and diamonds 40

Insects, lizards, and various animals were popular motifs from the '70s onwards 40

A fine example of the diamond floral spray with delicate setting 40

Queen Victoria. By Lady Abercrombie, after Heinrich von Angeli 45

A bracelet by Castellani 46

Floral design in mosaic work 46

Enamel brooch by Giuliano, set with diamonds, pearls, and carbuncles 46

7

Banded agate drops in granulated settings with matching
    ear-rings   *page* 55
Necklace of gold pendant drops and gold brooches   56
An amethyst and gilt necklace   61
Enamelled brooch and three rings   61
A pearl and diamond gold brooch in the Neo-Classic manner   62
Finely enamelled pendant brooch and gold 'padlock' brooch   62
An example of saw-piercing, filigree, and engraved work   62
Amethysts set in a formal gold cartouche   62
Turquoise and pearl suite   67
Two brooches, topaz and gold floral bracelet, and pearl and
    amethyst pendant ear-rings   67
Ear piercing. A contemporary print, after E. R. Cooper   68
Necklace and ear-rings in gold set with emeralds, rubies, and
    pearls   77
Two necklaces with ear-rings *en suite*   77
Gold brooch, and necklace and ear-rings in gold with peridots
    in diamond surrounds   78
Pearl, amethyst, and gold brooch, and pearl crescent brooch   78
Amethyst and pearl brooch, and pearl and diamond brooch in
    gold   78
Gold and turquoise bracelet   83
A cluster of Victorian rings   83
The minuterie of the era: stick pins, small brooches, and gold
    chain purse   83
An early amethyst necklace set in gold   84
A brilliant-cut almandine garnet star pendant   84
A typical coral suite of the type fashionable in the mid-century   89
A fine opal and diamond necklace   90
Garnet bracelet and a typical *cabochon* garnet brooch   90
The tortoise, a motif popular in the 1880s   99
Gold brooch set with pearls   99
Gold brooch with 'blooming' and repoussé work   99
Amethyst, diamond, and pearl ring, and amethyst and filigree
    gold brooch   99
Simple link bracelet set with finely matched topaz   100
Gold brooches and gold link bracelet with pearls and ame-
    thysts   100

Illustrations

Gold and mollusc shell cameo suite *page* 105

Amethysts mounted in delicate filigree gold settings 105

Topaz in the heavy, opulent setting of the mid-Victorian
period 106

Gold bangle set with half pearls, two gold stud ear-rings, and
flexible gold bracelet set with carbuncles 106

Three pieces of A. W. N. Pugin jewellery 111

Presidential badge and chain by Alfred Gilbert, 1901 112

A well-made necklace and brooch designed by Arthur Gaskin,
1908 121

Brooch and pendant by C. R. Ashbee, *c.* 1900 122

Queen Victoria. By Bertha Muller, after Heinrich von Angeli 127

Small work and minuterie by the House of Fabergé 128

Do you see this Ring?
                        'Tis Rome-work, made to match
(By Castellani's imitative craft)
Etrurian circlets found, some happy morn,
After a dropping April; found alive
Spark-like 'mid unearthed slope-side figtree-roots
That roof old tombs at Chiusi: soft, you see,
Yet crisp as jewel-cutting

ROBERT BROWNING
The Ring and the Book, 1868

Preface

A PREFACE is often something in the nature of an apology. In it the author sets down what he has tried to do, and then excuses himself for his shortcomings. This is no exception.

The difficulty about the Victorian period for the historian or the research student is that it is over-documented. Normally a great deal of the historian's labour—and this is especially so if he is dealing with a minor craft like jewellery—consists in dredging old documents, memoirs, and letters for the occasional reference to the subject in which he is interested. It is not unlike looking for a needle in the proverbial haystack. From the 1830s onwards, however, the position is completely changed. Periodicals and magazines proliferate. Trade and industrial exhibitions, both in England and on the Continent, give rise to catalogues, exhibition reviews, and even governmental reports. Writers on art and aesthetics, like Mrs Haweis, and journalists, like George Augustus Sala, provide us with the contemporary view of fashions in dress and ornament. Trade magazines make their appearance, as well as journals designed especially for women.

The historian's task, on the surface, would appear to have been made much easier for him; in fact, it has become no easier but has only changed. He no longer has to search for his material, but has the equally arduous task of selection and discrimination. A fully-documented volume on 19th-century jewellery would require hundreds of pages—and make very dull reading. A chapter might well be written on the Whitby jet-cutting industry alone, and another on the mollusc-shell cameo and coral-carving industry of Italy.

In this survey of the craft of the jeweller during the Victorian period, I have attempted to chart only the main stream of fashion and technical change. When an aspect of jewellery has struck me as being particularly worthy of the student's and collector's attention —such as granulated and filigree gold-work—I have devoted space to an analysis of both its technical and aesthetic aspects. On the other hand, what seem to me aberrations of taste, like human-hair jewellery, I have been content to dismiss in a sentence. Inevitably, where a subject requires this exercise of choice and discrimination, it is the writer's own taste and judgment which are on trial.

The illustrations are not intended as an index of jewellery during the 19th century, but as an anthology rather. The majority of the pieces have been selected not because they are especially rare or unusual, but chiefly as examples of good-quality Victorian jewellery such as is available on the market at the present day. A certain number of museum pieces have been included, either because they are illustrative of techniques or of styles which are dealt with in the text.

For permission to illustrate pieces of jewellery and for assistance and co-operation in several ways, I am indebted to so many private collectors, as well as curators of public collections, that I can do no more than indicate those without whose help this work could not have been undertaken: the authorities of the British Museum, the Victoria and Albert Museum, the National Portrait Gallery, the National Gallery, and the Worshipful Company of Goldsmiths. Among the many antique dealers and jewellers who have loaned me pieces for examination or photography, I would especially like to thank Messrs Harvey and Gore, Asprey and Company, Wartski and Company, S. J. Phillips, Richard Ogden, Cameo Corner, Biggs of Farnham, Garrard and Company, and Carrington and Company.

I am particularly indebted to the Editor of the *Watchmaker, Jeweller, and Silversmith* for allowing me to make use of material from his magazine, which was founded in 1875 and has accordingly been invaluable for the history of the Late Victorian period. I am indebted also to Miss Judith Banister, F.G.A., who not only placed her gemmological knowledge at my disposal but assisted in the selection of many of the illustrations. Finally I would like to record my indebtedness to the late Mr R. W. Symonds, F.S.A., F.R.I.B.A., for having allowed me to make use of his unrivalled collection of books dealing with the 19th-century arts and crafts.

E. B.

The Eighteenth-century Background

THE termination of centuries and the reigns of monarchs, although they are often used by historians as convenient water-tight boxes, very rarely provide exact lines of demarcation. This is particularly true when one comes to consider such shifting and complex matters as the tides of fashion and taste. Jewellery, a craft and not a pure art, is even more subject than similar crafts, such as those of the silversmith and the woodworker, to the movements of fashion. One cannot consider the course and trend of jewellery during the 19th century without taking at least a cursory look at the century which preceded it.

The 18th century in terms of jewellery has been called the 'Age of the Faceted Stone', for it was during this period that the principal changes in the centuries-old craft were made by the lapidary. Up to the 18th century, the setting and the mounting of a piece of jewellery had played as important a part, if not more so, than the gemstones themselves. With the discovery of the brilliant cut for diamonds at the close of the 17th century, however, a new era was ushered in. The technical achievements of the 18th-century lapidary and stone-cutter brought a revolution in taste and placed the emphasis on the gemstone. The work of the goldsmith, the enameller, and the gem-setter consequently declined.

The two principal forms of diamond cutting which played so important a part in Victorian jewellery were brought to a high degree of perfection during the 18th century. The earliest of these cuts, and one which the Victorian jeweller often preferred to its great successor, was the rose cut. In the most perfect form of rose

13

cutting, the diamond is covered with twenty-four triangular facets in the shape of a hemisphere. All these facets are arranged in a completely regular fashion, and the diamond is left with a flat base. The rose cut is an extremely attractive one and possesses a soft brilliance, though it is nowhere so 'alive' and sparkling as the brilliant cut. There are seven principal forms of the rose cut, some more elaborate than others, but all alike in the fact that the facets are hexagonally arranged and the base of the stone is flat.

The brilliant cut, which has been attributed to the 17th-century Venetian lapidary, Vincenti Peruzzi, was a descendant of the old table cut, and possessed a great many more facets than the rose. The modern brilliant, which has a larger table or top facet than the 18th- and 19th-century cuts, retains the same basic design, having thirty-three facets on the crown (the top half of the diamond) and twenty-five facets on the pavilion (the bottom half).

These were the two forms of diamond cutting which dominated the world of jewellery during the 18th century. They continued, together with some alterations and additions, to provide the basic cuts for the premier gemstone throughout the Victorian period.

Despite the fact that the Georgian period is often looked upon as the century *par excellence* in which England established her own styles in the arts and crafts, it remains a fact that jewellery, at any rate, was still dominated by the fashions of France. The peaks of excellence reached by the jewellers working for the French royal court could be emulated by the English craftsmen, but could not be excelled. The quality of London gem-cutting and mounting was as fine then as it has ever been, but the fashion which was followed usually emanated from the French court. One distinction, however, which marked English jewellers' work during this century was a refined classicism which made their products a little more austere than those of the Continent. Even foreign craftsmen resident in England, like the great silversmith, Paul de Lamerie, were influenced by this almost austere elegance. It was this fact which, in silverware as well as in jewellery, saved England from the more riotous excesses of Continental rococo.

An influx of foreign workmen and artisans during the 18th century proved beneficial to nearly all the crafts. These refugees from the oppressive governmental systems of Germany, France, and Italy injected a fine degree of Continental vitality into the techniques and styles of English jewellery. Lacombe, in his *Tableau de Londres* (1777), remarked on the number of foreign workmen employed in the city and concluded: 'La quantité d'ouvriers étrangers établis à Londres a produit une efflorescence utile au commerce, malgré le peu d'encouragement qu'ils reçoivent de la nation et des riches entrepreneurs, mais la misère et le despotisme Allemand et Français peuplera toujours cette Babilone. . . .'

The diamond and the faceted gemstone were the most important heritages bequeathed by the 18th century to its successor. So, too, was the feeling that Paris was, and seemed as if it would always be, the *arbiter elegantiarum*. This was perhaps surprising, for a country which has passed through a revolution and the extinction of its court and many of its nobility seems unlikely to remain the dictator of so essentially luxurious and frivolous an art as that of jewellery.

The immediate result of the French Revolution was, of course, the destruction of innumerable objects of *bijouterie* and *minuterie*, and a complete reaction against the fashionable excesses of the old court circle. For a time, but for a short time only, the fashion in French jewellery tended towards the very plain and simple— polished semi-precious or even ordinary stones set in unadorned gold or silver mounts.

During the Napoleonic period, however, the pendulum swung back again, and extravagances of faceted gemstones became fashionable. By the time that Queen Victoria acceded to the throne, Paris had once more resumed its place as the dictator of Europe's fashions. Even if France had remained a revolutionary republic, it is doubtful whether anything could for long have imposed a

Puritan's mask on the natural Gallic genius for decoration and adornment. Throughout the Victorian period, Paris was still regarded by the jewellers (as well as the dressmakers) of London as the dictator of fashion and good taste.

In another direction, quite apart from that taken by precious jewellery, the 18th century laid the foundations of the 19th. This was in the sphere of mass-produced, or what we would nowadays call 'costume', jewellery. Although, with the advent of new machinery and new technical processes, it was the 19th century which transformed the appearance of the lower-middle and lower classes (so that even the shop girl or factory worker could afford a brooch or a bangle), the foundations of this mass-produced jewellery had been laid long before the close of the 18th century.

The growth of Birmingham from a small town into the head-quarters of the silver- and metal-work industries was extremely rapid. Matthew Boulton was one of the men who played a major part in this development of Birmingham's industry, and as early as 1771, when the articles of the Birmingham Metal Company were signed, the growth of Birmingham's mass-produced jewellery industry was assured. Matthew Boulton's factories were producing, among many other wares, cut-steel jewellery and plated jewellery long before the end of the century. By 1790, so great was the demand of the jewellery and metal-work industries of the city, that over one-third of the total output of the Cornish mines was reserved for Birmingham.

The technical improvements in the glass-making industry during the 18th century paved the way for the large-scale production of paste for jewellery. Furthermore, the increasing prosperity of the English middle classes created a market for shoe-buckles, brooches, and bracelets set with paste in emulation of the diamond and precious-stone jewellery of the well-to-do. In the 19th century the electro-plating of base metals opened a way for the production of cheap jewellery with a gilt or silver finish, but even this had to some

Victoriana. With the exception of the brooch in the foreground, this is a
representative group of minor 19th-century pieces.

A tiara in gold, set with diamonds and pearls. First half of the 19th century.

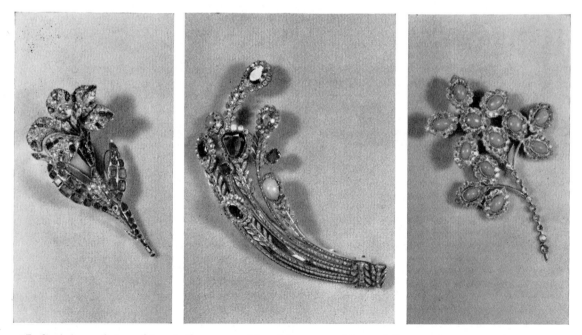

(*Left*) A brooch in gold and silver, set with rubies, emeralds, and diamonds. (*centre*) An aigrette in gold set with diamonds and turquoise. (*Right*) A brooch in gold set with diamonds and turquoise.

extent been anticipated by the 'ingenious Mr Pinchbeck', whose formula for a pseudo-gold had for some time enabled the less wealthy to possess articles that in previous centuries would have been outside the range of their purses.

In Sheffield, Thomas Bolsover had discovered the fusion of silver and copper—a discovery which gave rise to the Sheffield Plate industry. By 1760, Horace Walpole could comment that Sheffield was 'one of the foulest towns in England in the most charming situation, where there are 22,000 inhabitants making knives and scissors'. But, as well as knives and scissors, Sheffield was producing buttons and buckles, mounts for cameos, watchcases, and chatelaines.

Apart from the technical and mechanical improvements which the 18th century bequeathed to the Victorian jeweller, there were a number of fashions that were revived during the succeeding century. Prominent among these was the *parure*, the suite of matching jewellery which might contain necklace, bracelet, earrings, and brooch. The *Sévigné*, a bodice ornament or brooch lavishly set with stones in gold or silver, was another 18th-century style which continued in favour throughout the Victorian period. Mourning jewellery was another. Lockets and brooches decorated with funerary scenes, and rings enamelled with the initials and dates of the loved one, were not, as is sometimes supposed, a Victorian contribution to jewellery. The Queen's long widowhood and lengthy period of mourning undoubtedly aided the popularity of mourning jewellery during the 19th century, but the vogue for this funereal style had long been established.

The fact that the craft of the jeweller did not decline during the Victorian era was in part due to the continuance of the high standard demanded by the apprenticeship system. Then, as now, the Wardens of Goldsmiths Hall watched over their trade with scrupulous regard for fine craftsmanship and integrity. The apprenticeship system was a rigorous one, but it served to maintain a high standard throughout the difficulties and troubles of the Industrial Revolution. The jeweller was always something of an aristocrat among craftsmen, and even the lowering of standards during the Victorian period was never able to reduce him from craftsman to artisan—as was the case in some of the other crafts, such as that of the furniture or cabinet maker.

In all branchès of the crafts, classical art and motifs dominated the last twenty-five years of the 18th century. The discoveries at Herculaneum and Pompeii reinforced this prevailing classicism. It was a classicism that was to experience a notable revival during the Victorian period, under the auspices of such craftsmen as Castellani in Rome and Giuliano in London.

2

Early Victorian and High Victorian Styles

THE influence of the Romantic Movement dominates all Early Victorian jewellery. Like the major arts, the crafts reacted against the prevailing classicism of the 18th century and flowered into colourful mediaeval and Gothic forms. The novels of Sir Walter Scott and the poetry of Lord Byron combined in the popular imagination with the extravagant fantasies of the Gothic novel to produce a revolution in dress and fashion.

The early years of the century were still marked by the simplicity of the clothes, the lightness of materials, and the comparative poverty of the jewellery that had accompanied the French Revolution. Flimsy muslins, lawns, and batistes were not materials suitable for heavy brooches or elaborate ornament, and the 'citoyenne' styles of France were still copied in the predominantly aristocratic society of England. The reaction against the Grecian mode, when it came, was extreme. Small slashed sleeves made their appearance, ruffs were worn and fashion looked back nostalgically to the Middle Ages, and—in England—to the Tudors.

For formal occasions *parures* set with diamonds were revived at the court of the Emperor Napoleon. For ordinary daytime wear *parures* set with semi-precious stones became popular. This was a fashion that was to last right through the century. Flower, wheat, and barley-ear motifs were widely used for diamond jewellery during the 1820s and 1830s.

With the Restoration in France, the classical styles in fashion gave way to the romantic. In England the revival of the Gothic coincided with these changes on the Continent. Gothic forms, which played so large a part in furniture and architecture during this period, and the importance of which can be judged from an examination of Loudon's *Encyclopaedia of Cottage, Villa, and Farm Architecture* (1833), were also prominent in the metal-work and jewellery of the time. The influence of Pugin and his followers on the arts and crafts of this period must also not be underestimated. A minor revival of enamelling took place, and brooches and pendants were designed to catch the new 'period flavour' of the clothes and hair styles.

The great French jeweller, Froment-Meurice, was probably the first designer and craftsman of any note to make use of these contemporary mediaeval motifs in jewellery, although he was soon followed by London, as well as Parisian, jewellers. The *ferronière*, a brow ornament that took its name from Leonardo da Vinci's portrait of '*La Belle Ferronière*', was one of the more marked examples of this romantic revolution. During the Renaissance, when the height and whiteness of a woman's brow was considered one of the most important desiderata for beauty, such an ornament had served its purpose by calling attention to a noble forehead. In the 19th century it was something of an anachronism. By the 1840s the simple hair styles that had made the wearing of a *ferronière* possible had given place to a more romantic fashion. Hair was twisted upwards from the nape of the neck, arranged in formal loops, and held in place with combs. Very often a few ringlets were arranged so as to hang in mock disorder over one cheek.

By the 1850s the Romantic Movement, though still flourishing, had passed its peak, and we find it sharing equal place with the 'naturalistic'—itself, of course, an offshoot of Rousseau's insistence on 'Back to Nature'. The one thread which links together all the crafts at the Great Exhibition of 1851 is the accent on

Seven silver sprays set with diamonds and (*centre*) a gold diamond-set brooch.

23

Necklace and ear-rings *en suite*, of silver and gold set with diamonds and sapphires.

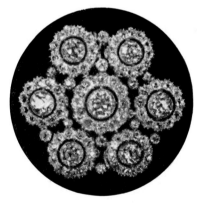

(*Left*) Gold floral brooch set with diamonds, rubies, and emeralds. (*Above*) A star cluster brooch of diamonds set in silver.

24

'naturalistic' or faithful representation. Gothic and mediaeval forms and motifs were widely represented, but the treatment of woodcarving, silver, metal-work, and jewellery was predominantly naturalistic.

A typical display at the Great Exhibition was that of Hunt and Roskell, whose pieces clearly show the blend of naturalism and romanticism prevalent at the time:

A diamond bouquet, being a specimen of the art of diamond setting. The flowers: the anemone, rose, carnation, etc., are modelled from nature. This ornament divides into seven different sprigs, each complete in design, and the complicated flowers, by mechanical contrivances, separate for the purpose of effectual cleaning. It contains nearly 6,000 diamonds, the largest of which weighs upwards of ten carats, and some of the smallest in the stamens of the flowers would not exceed 1000th part of a carat.

Enamelled portrait of Her Majesty, on gold, by J. Haslem, after F. Winterhalter, painted by His Royal Highness Prince Albert's permission, from a picture in his possession. The portrait is surrounded with a wreath of oak, enamelled on fine gold, set with pearls and diamonds.

Ornament for the hair, composed of branch coral, connected by leaves of enamel and gold, enriched with diamonds.

Several brooches and other ornaments in enamelled gold, set with diamonds. The flowers modelled from nature.

Enamelled portrait of Her Majesty, on gold, by J. Haslem, set as a bracelet, with carbuncles and diamonds.

Specimens of ear-rings in emeralds, diamonds, carbuncles, etc., after the marbles from Nineveh.

Enamelled portrait of Shakespeare, on gold, by W. Essex, from a portrait in the possession of the Earl of Ellesmere, set as a ring with diamonds.

The accent on enamelled pieces should be noted as well as the use of coral—already on a decline by this date—and the naturalistic modelling of the flowers.

The publication by Sir Austen Henry Layard in 1848 of *Nineveh and its Remains* had as widespread an effect on the Victorian public as the discovery of Tutankhamen's tomb on the 20th century. In the same way that at the beginning of the century Baron Denon's *Voyage dans la Basse et la Haute Egypte* (1802) had made the whole of educated Europe conscious of the civilization and decorative arts of ancient Egypt, so Layard's book introduced Assyrian motifs into English jewellery and metal-work.

Sometimes clues like this—the production of a book, the discovery of an ancient civilization, or the invention of some new technique—can aid the student and historian in the dating of a piece of jewellery. Pieces with distinctly Assyrian themes are not common, and one can usually ascribe them with some confidence to the five years following the publication of Layard's book. At the same time, the dating of 19th-century jewellery is a task that cannot be undertaken with absolute confidence. So many old motifs were revived during this era, and so many new styles were being used concurrently, that the simple 'layer upon layer' technique which helps in dating the work of earlier centuries cannot be used without great discretion.

The position of the Victorian Arts and Crafts was well summed up by Sir Matthew Digby Wyatt, writing in the *Journal of Design* in 1851:

'In all former stages of society—in other periods of our own English History, and in other countries—production, in whatever branch, or under whatever sky, was self-interpreting, told its own story, and carried with it its own credentials. Its *where* and *when* were unmistakable. It needs but the veriest tyro in art to settle the date or the place of a church, or a medal, or a dagger, or a piece of earthenware, or a manuscript, or a jewel, or a fragment of embroidery, of metal-work, or of bookbinding. There is not a handwriting extant, of any antiquity, which even a slight familiarity with the subject would not readily assign to its century—perhaps to its city. But how stands the case among ourselves? We design and execute in every conceivable style. We imitate every extant school. We are equally at home in the reproduction of classical and of Byzantine art—Etruscan ware and Majolica; we can execute Chinese or Athenian with the same facility; we can forge —perhaps that is the most appropriate term—an Egyptian obelisk or a Corinthian capital, a so-called Gothic moulding, or a Sèvres cup. We are not just at present contending that all this is wrong— we only say that it is a fact, and a new fact . . .'

It is not that the collector or the student is likely to be deceived into thinking a piece of Victorian 'Gothic' enamelling or 'Renaissance' pendant are other than 19th century in manufacture. The regularity of the finish, and a certain mechanical coldness, for one thing, militate against them. The difficulty does arise, though, of placing within a decade or so pieces that are based on many borrowed styles. A Moorish or Turkish style, for instance, can sometimes be discerned in English and French pieces dating from the 1840s. The French motifs for such pieces were usually drawn from Algeria which recent events had brought into the public consciousness. The English, on the other hand, drew upon Byron's Albania and Turkey for themes that accorded with their romantic conceptions of *Lara* and the *Corsair*.

During the decade preceding the Great Exhibition, bodices were high and white collars were fashionable. Small brooches and lockets at the neck were considered suitable for daytime wear. The ears were usually concealed, for the fashionable hair style had the hair drawn back over the ears and made up into a bun. Evening dress, on the other hand, despite the prevailing modesty of the period, was *décolleté* and allowed for the display of lavish diamond necklaces. Diamonds of this period were often set in gold, with the visible or front area of the setting in highly polished silver.

It must be borne in mind that during the Victorian period few unmarried women wore jewellery. The signs of a husband's prosperity were to be seen in the jewels worn by his wife, but an unmarried daughter would at the most have a simple necklet of pearls. 'The most fashionable neck ornaments for a young girl,' we read in the trade journal, *The Watchmaker, Jeweller, and Silversmith* of 1875 (the year in which this magazine was founded), 'is undoubtedly a row of pearls. Few people are prepared to pay the number of pounds which a row of real pearls is worth; but there is an excellent imitation sold which almost defies detection by the expert. . . .' (For 19th-century imitation pearls, see page 82.)

By the close of the century, however, the restrictions which had governed women for so long were giving way, and this foretaste of emancipation was revealed in the small sphere of jewellery. In an issue of 1888, the editor of this same trade journal makes the following comment: 'We note a rather important innovation in fashion in respect to the wearing of diamonds. Henceforth their use is not to be entirely restricted to married women. In Paris unmarried girls are to be seen wearing small diamonds in their ears . . . the stones weigh about a sixteenth of a carat.'

By the middle of the 1850s, the crinoline was in fashion, and this revolution in style was accompanied by the use of heavier velvet materials. Heavier materials, as always in the history of jewellery, meant larger and more elaborate jewels. During the daytime ladies often wore their hair in nets, and a contemporary account reads: 'Even little girls of eight years old wear their hair in nets—not invisible nets, but very obvious silk nets, spangled with jet.' The crinoline and the use of heavier dress materials lasted for nearly fifteen years—the fifteen years during which so much of the jewellery which is instinctively hailed as 'Victorian' was produced.

It was during this Mid- or High Victorian period that jewellery assumed a sumptuous appearance. Settings tended to be heavy; much use was made of gold, coloured gold and 'bloomed' gold being popular. Coloured stones, particularly the amethyst and the topaz mounted as brooches, bracelets, and necklaces, were part of this prevailing richness. Cameos were fashionable. The true gemstone cameo—as opposed to the mollusc shell (see page 85)—has long formed one of the highlights of the lapidary's craft, and some of the Victorian examples are very fine. Renaissance and classical cameos were copied, and pastiches on these early themes were improvised.

Almost any hard precious or semi-precious stone will serve the cameo-cutter for his materials, and the Victorians used a wide range; amethysts and emeralds for the better-quality work, and garnet, agate, jasper, and haematite for lesser pieces.

Cameo and intaglio work differs from most lapidary work in that a stone which is in a sense 'imperfect' may well yield the best results. For normal lapidary work, which nowadays means bringing out the maximum beauty from a faceted stone, the more perfect the gemstone in the rough the better should be the finished article. In cameo and intaglio work, on the other hand, the lapidary can use faults of colour and imperfections of surface to improve his effects. In the same way, in the 16th century, jewellers improvised on the curious shapes of baroque pearls to produce some of their most inventive pieces.

The Victorian lapidary had one advantage over the craftsmen of earlier ages in that the wheel on which his work was done was power-operated. Apart from this, he worked with the same tools, and with a mixture of diamond- or sapphire-powder and oil, as had been the practice for centuries. In the days before mechanical power was available, the normal method for engraving and cutting the surface of a stone was for the gemstone to be held secure on the work-bench while the craftsman worked on it with a hand- or foot-operated drill. With the advent of mechanical power the modern technique was evolved of holding the gemstone on a 'gemstick' in the hand, and applying it to a rapidly revolving disc or wheel. By the close of the Victorian period experiments were being made in the even more modern technique of engraving gemstones with a power-operated dentist's drill fitted with suitable cutting heads.

Some of the Victorian cameo work was particularly fine, but it very rarely equalled the grace and delicacy of the French 18th-century masters. Intaglios dating from this period are not uncommon, for the Victorian man still found use for a signet-ring. This was one of the few pieces of jewellery which had been left in the masculine sphere after the revolutionary change in men's fashion during the Regency. Fobs and seals still lingered on, however, and the elaborate watch and chain, and the sovereign-case and the card-case, did not vanish until the 1914–18 war.

Elaborate stomachers and detachable jewellery were popular for formal wear by the 1860s. W. G. Deeley, who visited the Paris Exhibition of 1867 for the Society of Arts, had the following comments to make on the prevailing fashion and styles displayed there:

'Commencing with the necklaces, as the most expensive, I found some most elegant specimens in the Greek style, some of them large enough to cover the front of a lady's chest, and so arranged that the different pendant ornaments or drops, when detached, can be used either as a brooch, necklet, pendant ear-rings, or ornaments for the hair. I consider the manner of the construction very good, and, at the same time, very simple. The whole of the necklace can be joined together by means of hooks and screws that any one could manage. Most of the diamonds were set in silver, and a few in 18-carat gold, which I think is no improvement on the silver settings for large stones; yet an amalgamation of the two metals, silver for the brilliants and gold for the light ornamentation (which is generally set with rose diamonds), shows the character of the design much better, and, when judiciously used, has a very pretty effect . . . I was rather surprised at the almost total absence of the imitation of flowers, yet what there was was magnificent. A most complete sprig of lilac was a splendid specimen of what French taste and patience can accomplish, every flower and stem being as perfect as nature, and at the same time retaining plenty of strength. There was also a very nice imitation of a tulip, and most beautifully done it was too, the streaks of colour therein being set with rubies, emeralds, and sapphires, as near the natural shape and colour as it is possible to get them. The remainder of the tulip, as well as the leaves and stem, was set with brilliants and rose diamonds. The harmonising of the colours in this particular instance was really grand. There were also several imitations of birds, suitable either for brooches or ornaments for the hair. The first was a peacock, with spread tail, each eye in the feathers being supplied with an emerald; and a few also were placed on the breast; the rest of the body, as well as the feathers in the tail, was filled up with rose diamonds. There was also a small lyre bird, made of gold, and set all-over with diamonds, mostly rose-cut. The humming birds were very pretty and tastily made. The most peculiar point was this, the generality of them are set with rose diamonds, with emeralds or sapphires just on the front of the breast, and these so nicely painted and arranged as to give them all the appearance of nature itself.'

Sixteen years had gone by since the Great Exhibition, and yet the emphasis on naturalistic treatment was still as strong as ever. It will also be noticed that Grecian styles for formal jewellery were still fashionable. In secondary jewellery—pieces for daytime wear or set with semi-precious stones—the romantic influence was also still discernible. Hancock and Sons, for instance, were advertising at this time: 'Gems arranged and mounted in the Holbein style.'

For Court or evening wear, on the other hand, the trend was

more and more towards a lavish display of diamonds. By the end of the century the settings would become so light as to be almost invisible, but in the 1860s and 1870s the settings even for diamonds were comparatively heavy. Elaborate and heavy bracelets were another feature of the period. The following is a contemporary description of some typical examples—bracelets such as can still be found in second-hand jewellers' shops of London and the provinces:

'. . . a bulrush bracelet, with leaves coming up to the front, the cane going round, and soldered to the end of the rush, the leaves either nicely chased or enamelled, the rush roughly chased, and left dead from the colouring. To add still more to the beauty of the bracelet, a lizard, about two inches in length, set with rose diamonds, creeping up the leaves or a snake entwining itself around, making a very natural article [*sic*]. Another style of bracelet that looks very rich is a coil of gold tubing, consisting of about four twists, after the fashion of a large spring, made to take on and off the arm by means of wire springs and joints working inside the tubing. The front of the bracelet is enriched with diamonds, rubies, sapphires, and emeralds, ten of them, mounted in strong clawed collets, soldered to the tubes, and so arranged that, when placed on the arm, it forms a variegated check pattern. The gold is 18 carat and all of it is polished bright. In some instances the jewellers are trying to introduce a fine green gold leaf, chased, running down a bangle-bracelet, polished bright, with a small hollow, about an eighth of an inch from the edge, just wide enough to admit the green gold ornamentation . . .'

Throughout the century a comparison between English and French work establishes the fact that, although they were often similar in style and techniques, French pieces tended towards a greater elegance and lightness. The English jeweller maintained his affection for romantic themes long after these had been discarded on the Continent and a second 'Greek Revival' had set in.

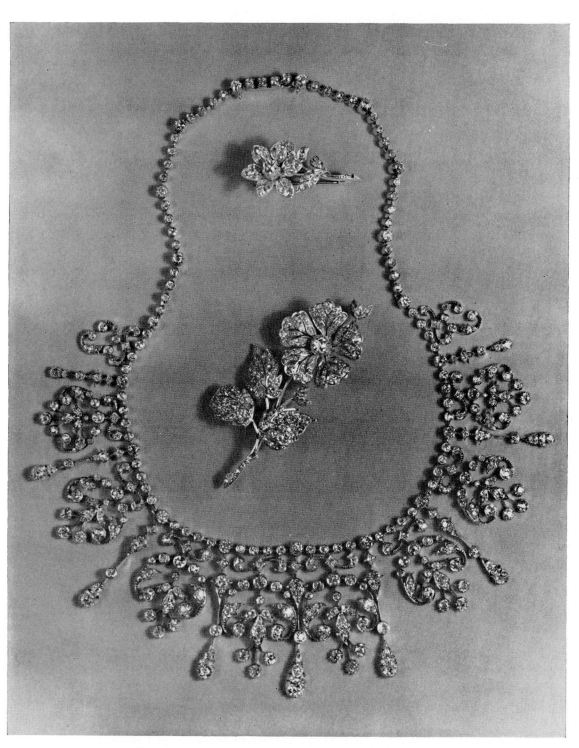

Diamond open-work necklace with two floral sprays.

(*Left*) Early Victorian diamond and ruby brooch with emerald centre.
(*Below*) Early Victorian open-work scroll brooch. The diamonds are pavé and collet-set brilliants, with a rose diamond in the centre.

(*Above*) The High Victorian style—a gold brooch set with large amethysts.
(*Right*) Delicate gold filigree work in a butterfly brooch set with opals and other gemstones.

34

'I am afraid,' wrote George Augustus Sala, 'that for elegance, lightness, and brilliance, we cannot beat the Parisian *joaillier*.' This distinction between English and French jewellery of the period is brought out by James Pamplin, a working jeweller of Birmingham, in his *Report on the Jewellery and Gilt Toy Trade*:

'A principal feature of French designs is the prevalence of Greek ornament which, from its beauty of form, combined with evenness of outline, is peculiarly adapted to the jeweller. The few specimens in Roman, and the still fewer in Elizabethan ornament, from their excellence prove that their resources have been very much overlooked.

'The ornamentation of the French is characteristic from its variety; lapping, engraving, chasing, and enamelling being frequently introduced into one article. In general work, enamel is but sparingly employed, but in the elaboration of works of art is more skilfully applied than by any other nation.

'In construction the French work is superior in lightness, the metal, even in the common work, being regarded more as an accessory than otherwise. In fine diamond work no nation exhibits productions of equal lightness to some of M. Rouvenat . . .

'The design of the (English) gold-work is heavy and inartistic, but we believe it to be the production of professional designers, though of indifferently educated art-workmen. The ornamentation is very slight, seldom more than one kind upon an article, and the general appearance is rich and massive.'

James Pamplin then singles out the work of Brogden, H. Emmanuel, Hancock and Sons, and Hunt and Roskell as being of the highest standard in England at the time.

The extract, however, is sufficient to show that the English jeweller was still enamoured of gold-work and massive ornate jewellery. The French, on the other hand, were already by the 1870s paving the way for what was to be the distinguishing feature of late Victorian jewellery—its elegance and its delicacy.

The great change in Victorian fashion, both in dress and in its ornament, began in 1870. By the mid-sixties the death of the crinoline had been announced with the introduction of a folding crinoline. The year 1870 saw the appearance of the style which was to dominate the rest of the century. Skirts now became bunched up in a bustle at the back, and dress materials became extremely varied so that it was not rare to find bodice, skirt, overskirt, and trimmings all of different materials and even of different colours.

Hair styles altered at the same time, long hair designed to fall in curls from the crown of the head to the shoulders becoming fashionable. This meant that the ears were now uncovered, and the ear-ring, which had been suffering from an eclipse, came back into favour. Large pendant ear-rings of every type and description were made in great numbers during the next twenty years. In the last decade there was an inevitable reaction against them, and ear-rings practically disappeared until, at the close of the century, the popularity of the Creole ear-ring brought about another revival.

The close of the High Victorian period was marked by a number of Oriental or Indian influences on jewellery and metal-work. These became particularly noticeable in the years immediately after 1876—the year in which the Queen became Empress of India. Oriental designs in engraved work, a lavish use of coloured gemstones, filigree silver, and silver wire-work, all date from this period.

The third great archaeological influence of the period was provided by the discoveries of Dr Schliemann in Greece and Asia Minor. The *Album of the Arts and Industries of Great Britain*, published in 1887 to mark Her Majesty's Jubilee, has the following comment:

'The excavations made by Dr Schliemann in Homer's city of Troy, in Mycenae, and throughout the Troad, are too recent to have escaped the memory of any, and the glorious results of his researches and his discoveries on the site of these ancient cities will probably live for all time. The remains of pottery, of jewellery, and of endless other relics of a bygone age unearthed by the famous excavator, have excited a deep interest in the minds of men, which fact our manufacturers were not slow to recognise. Hence they made most praiseworthy and successful attempts to copy, reproduce, and adapt them to ornaments and to articles of jewellery for the adornment of the present generation. These consist of silver, but are oxydised to imitate more closely the antique specimens from which they are copied, and some of the figures are inlaid with pure gold, and bear mottoes in Greek of friendship and love . . .'

Archaeological discoveries played an important part in shaping the design of jewellery and metal-work throughout the Victorian era. The desire for knowledge and self-improvement that played so large a part in middle-class Victorian life led to 'antiquarian jewellery' acquiring a distinct *cachet* of its own. The firm of Backes and Strauss, we learn, 'manufacture facsimiles of every description of ancient artistic work, and thus we find specimens of old Roman, Damascene, Renaissance, Rococo, and almost every distinct type of jewellery from all countries and all ages'.

By 1887 we find that, in precious jewellery at any rate, the Late Victorian or Early Edwardian style is becoming dominant. Settings are becoming somewhat lighter, and the faceted stone has almost won its battle against the enameller and the goldsmith. In the sphere of secondary or daytime jewellery, however, this was not the case, and the styles remained opulent and ostentatious. Necklaces, bracelets, brooches, hair ornaments, and ear-rings were lavish with colour and designed to be noticed. Snake bracelets remained popular, and there is a description of a 'coil bracelet possessing such elasticity as to enable it to be readily put on and taken off without the use of any snap or fastening and, at the same time, fitting any arm to perfection . . . in the form of a snake, this bracelet has become an article of great demand.'

In the first fifty years of Queen Victoria's reign the industry had expanded immensely. It was true that high-class London jewellers still tended to look to Paris for a lead in fashion, but in the sphere of popular and semi-precious jewellery Birmingham led the way. This city was now exporting 'gilt toys', imitation jewellery, plated ware, enamels, and all types of minuterie to nearly every country in Europe, as well as to the British colonies and possessions overseas. A review of the Birmingham *Jewellery Manufacture* (1887) states:

'In this branch of industry, as in many others, the year 1887 formed as it were a landmark, and it is during the half-century which has elapsed that the local trade has made marvellous strides of progress. The scale on which the manufacture of gold and silver-smith's work is now carried on in Birmingham may be inferred approximately from the fact that bullion to the value of about £1,100,000 is annually thus used there.'

On this note it seems fitting to leave the High Victorian period and turn to a consideration of some of the outstanding products of the century.

(*Above*) Pavé and collet-set rose and brilliant diamonds form a classic formal spray. (*Right*) Top left, a floral spray. Top right, brilliant and rose diamonds surround a fine briolette. Lower left, a floral spray with diamonds and rubies. Lower right, a diamond crescent set with brilliants. (Fashionable in the 18th century, the crescent survived right through to the Edwardian period.)

(*Left*) A large mixed-cut cairngorm surrounded by pearls and garnets. (*Right*) The rising-sun motif. Rose and brilliant diamonds in silver.

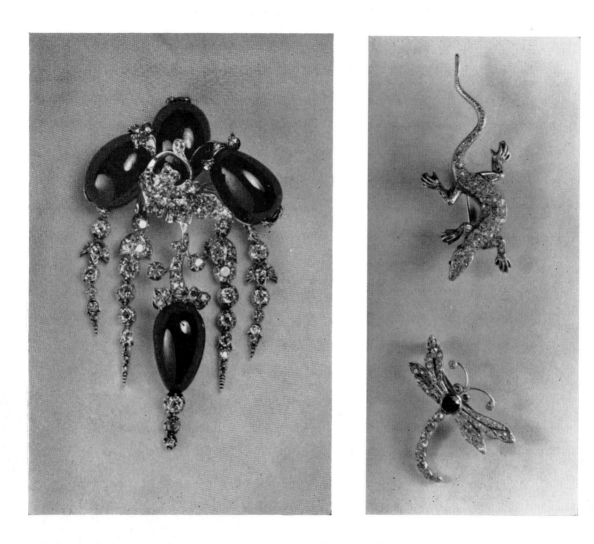

(*Above left*) Opulence was the keynote of the High Victorian period: carbuncles and diamonds. (*Above right*) Insects, lizards, and various animals were popular motifs from the '70s onwards.

A fine example of the diamond floral spray with delicate setting. Late Victorian.

Gold Filigree Jewellery and the Etruscan Style

ONE of the most interesting facets of the jeweller's craft during the 19th century is the Etruscan style or the use of granulated gold. The achievements of Victorian craftsmen in this medium were superb, and must count among the few real advances made in jewellery since the discovery of the brilliant cut for diamonds.

The 19th-century fashion in jewellery, as we have seen, had been profoundly influenced by the first achievements of professional archaeology—the excavations at Pompeii. Although the excavations at Herculaneum in the middle of the 18th century had aroused great interest throughout Europe and had produced many motifs which were incorporated in the classical revival, it was the new discoveries at Pompeii that really gave rise to the enormous vogue for the antique. It was between 1806 and 1814 that the extent of the ruins and the artistic treasures of the devastated city were largely uncovered, under the stimulus and enthusiasm of the French Government. For almost the first time since the Renaissance, artists and craftsmen were suddenly confronted with the crafts of the classical past in the shape of a host of unique and beautiful articles—many of them of a minor nature like jewellery. The influences of the Pompeian mural paintings alone cannot be over-estimated in tracing the history of the crafts during the 19th century.

French jewellers were, somewhat naturally, the first to profit by these designs and decorations, and almost immediately established a vogue for imitation mosaic work in items of jewellery. The native Italian craftsmen were not slow to follow their lead, and lastly—deriving their inspiration at second-hand from Paris— came the jewellers in England.

As a reaction against the somewhat plain and heavy pieces made in the Directoire style, the new elegance, lightness, and colour of the Neo-Classical revival enjoyed a wide popularity. One of the aspects of ancient technique and craftsmanship which fascinated the 19th-century artists was the supreme delicacy of the gold-work. The fineness of the minute gold beads and airy filigree came as something like a revelation to craftsmen who, for too long, had been dominated by the concept of jewellery as a display of faceted stones linked by inconspicuous silver settings.

The whole history of jewellery in the Western world may be roughly defined as a pendulum-like movement between the setting (the work of the *bijoutier*) and the precious stone (the work of the *joaillier*). In the closing years of the 17th century the discovery of the brilliant cut for the diamond had initiated one of these swings of the pendulum, and the 18th century was dominated by the glories of the faceted stone. It was high time then for a reaction, and the discoveries of the classical achievements in gold-work at Pompeii provided just the necessary stimulus.

It was in 1814, when this revival of the antique was sweeping all before it, that an Italian jeweller named Fortunato Pio Castellani opened up a small business in Rome. Like most goldsmiths and jewellers of the time, Castellani was enthusiastic about the classical revival, but whereas the majority were prepared to accept Roman craftsmanship as the main stream of true excellence, Castellani was determined to find the fountain-head. It seemed to him that not even the most delicate Roman work could compare with the minute precision in gold-work of the early Etruscans—a race whose origins are still somewhat in dispute, but whose jewellery and gold-work seems definitely to stem from the Greeks.

In the course of his studies, Castellani heard a rumour that in certain small villages in Umbria there were still local craftsmen working in gold in a traditional manner that had remained unchanged throughout the centuries. He examined some of the pieces reputed to come from this area, and saw at once that these craftsmen appeared to work with minute applications of granulated gold (*granaglia*) in a way that no Roman workmen of the time could equal. Finally, in St Angelo de Vado, a small out-of-the-way village in the Umbrian Marches, he found some of these native craftsmen. He induced them to come to Rome, and set them up as instructors to his own workmen. This small beginning led to the emergence throughout Europe of a completely new style of gold-work—the so-called Etruscan filigree style.

Castellani himself was more of an enthusiastic antiquarian than a great creative jeweller, and the pieces which in the early days came from his workshop were—as far as he could make them—authentic reproductions of Etruscan gold-work. He even marketed them under the somewhat alarming and, by modern advertising standards, uninspiring trade name of 'Italian Archaeological Jewellery'. In 1851 Castellani retired from business, and it was not until 1858, when his talented son Augusto resumed the reproduction of antique jewellery in considerable quantity, that the influence of the new discoveries in gold-work became widespread. English travellers in Rome soon became acquainted with the marvellous delicacy of this Italian jewellery, and it was not long before London, as well as Paris, began to blossom with imitators of the Castellani manner.

A good description of the effect produced by the display of this Etruscan-style jewellery is given by the Victorian journalist, George Augustus Sala, in his *Notes and Sketches of the Paris Exhibition of 1867*:

'The Castellani exhibit is of a duplex nature. The first category is formed of that wonderfully beautiful "Etruscan" jewellery, from antique models, in the production of which he has long held the first rank among Continental goldsmiths. The characteristics of this ware I have already described, as accurately as was in my power, in the notice of the goods shown by Mr Phillips of Cockspur Street. Among Castellani's special examples of Etruscan art, the most prominent is a sumptuously-worked coronal, or diadem of "decussated" and "reticulated" gold—an extraordinary specimen of design and workmanship, which has been purchased by the Earl of Dudley, at the price, I believe, of a thousand guineas. I much doubt whether the intrinsic value of this ornament exceeds a hundred pounds; but there cannot be any cause for complaint in the price asked and paid. The marvellous excellence of the workmanship would warrant the exaction of even a higher price than that quoted.

'The second moiety of M. Castellani's display is devoted to a very curious and suggestive collection of the gold and silver ornaments worn by the Italian peasantry and lower middle classes—ornaments which are rarely seen in the shops of fashionable Italian jewellers, but which form the principal stock-in-trade of the dealers who keep the poky little shops on the Ponte Vecchio at Florence, and in that sombre colonnade at the southern foot of the Rialto at Venice. Among the queer, coarse trinkets brought together by M. Castellani are great knobbed silver pins not much smaller than life preservers, and others, in the forms of daggers, arrows, anchors, and javelins, to transfix the "back hair" of the Contadini. There are bracelets as heavy as handcuffs, brooches like frying pans, and lockets as big as hand mirrors. The ear-rings are especially exorbitant, and of amazing variety of quaint and uncouth design.'

It was not only the granulated Etruscan work of Castellani which exerted a profound influence on the Victorian jeweller. Those heavy bracelets and 'knobbed silver pins' were also widely copied, so that side by side—from the same Italian source—was derived a vogue for minute and detailed workmanship, and a vogue

Queen Victoria. By Lady Abercrombie, after Heinrich von Angeli.

45

Floral design in mosaic work. The brooch is set in gold, with dolphins as supporters.

Enamel brooch by Giuliano, set with diamonds, pearls, and carbuncles.

A bracelet by Castellani, showing exceptionally fine Florentine mosaic work with granulated surrounds.

for the heavy, ostentatious peasant work of the Campagna. This was one of the first occasions in the history of the craft in Europe that the peasant jewellery of Europe had affected the fashions of the *salons*.

The exact techniques employed by the Castellani workmen have never to this day been divulged, but the fact that a number of first-class English and French jewellers were soon able almost to rival them suggests that, in principle, the methods of fabricating this fine standard of granulated gold-work were not so very different from those described by Cellini in his *Treatises*, or by the mediaeval monk-jeweller, Theophilus, in his *Schedula Diversarium Artium*. The best established antique method of making *granaglia*—that is, granulated metal—was to take gold or silver cuttings and heat them in a crucible. The cuttings were put in the crucible together with fine-powdered charcoal, and the crucible was rotated during the melting process. This rotary action caused the particles of gold or silver to roll in the charcoal and to take on a spherical shape. Finally, the charcoal was washed away, leaving the melted metal granules to be sorted for size.

Yet another method used for making gold or silver spheres was the beading tool, which is described by Theophilus as a block cut in two, with slots in the upper and lower half designed to form various patterns and sizes of beads. Gold or silver wire was then laid down along the centre of the beading tool, and the two halves were bound and hammered together, thus forcing the wire to take the imprint of the patterned grooves. The beads formed by this method were likely to be coarser and less precise in their shape than those made in a crucible, but it was simpler and quicker for certain types of work and, indeed, is sometimes still used today. (For a more technical examination of the processes of making granulated gold, see Chapter 6.)

Foremost of the 19th-century jewellers to copy the Castellani type of work was that distinguished craftsman, Fontenay of Paris, and many of his pieces found their way across the Channel. Meanwhile in England two native jewellers, Robert Phillips and John Brogden, were quick to follow the new mode and produced between them a great number of necklaces, brooches, and ear-rings, using settings of fine granulated gold. Also a Neapolitan, Carlo Giuliano, who had settled in London and who proudly called himself the heir of the great Italian tradition, began the production of fine gold-work in the new manner.

Giuliano's work, examples of which are still extant, is in the highest tradition of the goldsmith's craft. There is every justification for saying that many of his pieces were minor works of art. Giuliano's pieces, as fine and delicate in their workmanship as those of the Castellani family, have a graceful quality all their own. They benefited, probably, from the fact that he tied himself less to the classic originals, merely using similar techniques while working with contemporary themes.

In 1867 the Society of Arts sent a select committee of English craftsmen to the Paris Exhibition to study and report on the styles, methods, and techniques of the French and other foreign exhibitors. This interesting and worthwhile enterprise was prompted chiefly by the uneasy feeling, prevalent in England at the time, that all was not well with English standards of design. These reports were subsequently published by the Society, and make interesting reading, not least the report of W. G. Deeley, a working jeweller of Birmingham, whose opinions on the work of Castellani confirm Sala's impressions, but are all the more pertinent because they are those of a practising craftsman.

'Coming to the things made by Castellani,' he writes, '(there) was a coronet in the pure Byzantine style, its upper edge decorated with discs, these discs were placed at a short distance from each other, the discs had "cornice" edges. A necklace of very great beauty was also shown; it was composed of chains, pendants, a profusion of beads and filigree pippins; this was in the most beautiful Italian-Greek style. There was also another coronet to match the necklace. The examination of these things carries a conviction to the mind, and demonstrates the great utility, the abundantly suggestive character of the collection of ornaments worn by the peasantry of Italy, known as the "Castellani Collection" and purchased by the British Government.*

'To return to the modern exhibits of Castellani, the filigree was very good, also some antique rings; the generality of these stones were engraved and mounted very plain indeed. The stones used in these were as follows: the red cornelian, the striped onyx, the cat's eye, the lapis lazuli, and the chrysoprase, in different shapes; but instead of the oval-formed stone going up the finger, it is placed to stand across; a beautiful wreath for the hair like unto a laurel, leaving no fault to be found with the workmanship; the berries were formed of selected pearls, the leaves of gold, nicely formed, and, in fact, about the best representation of nature I ever remember seeing in such magnitude.'

One can discern, through the incoherence of this workman's prose style, a very genuine excitement and enthusiasm. What is noticeable is that it is not only the craftsmanship upon which he comments, but the use of such lesser gemstones as the cornelian and lapis lazuli. In the last quarter of the 19th century such stones were to be liberally employed in English work, but there seems little doubt that some of the impetus which brought them into popularity was derived from the successes of the Italian jewellers. That Brogden and Phillips were already successfully imitating the Castellani manner is evidenced by a further comment made by W. G. Deeley:

'Mr Brogden also shows a most peculiar taste [sic], and I think a most desirable one, for he has shown to the world a class of goods unequalled, and the manner in which he has treated the ancient styles is something wonderful. The enamelling is remarkable for the colours displayed and its general finish; any one could easily spend

*Now in the British Museum.

an hour or so at this case in examining the different things, as they are alike pleasing, and at the same time very interesting. Attached to each of the articles are small tickets explaining the history of the things imitated. Thanks are due to this gentleman for his thoughtfulness in doing so. The same can be said of Mr Phillips, of Cockspur Street, London, who has achieved a name that will make him famous throughout the world, and well deserving of it he is too, for his wonderful perseverance in endeavouring to place before the trade a series of ideas fit to be imitated by anyone; I don't say copied.'

But copied they were—as well as imitated—and the second-hand jewellers' shops of England still reveal innumerable attempts that aped the modes initiated by Castellani, and were successfully followed by Giuliano, Phillips, Brogden, and Hunt and Roskell.

The question is sometimes raised as to how to distinguish 19th-century work made in imitation of the antique from the originals. In fact there is little difficulty, for the 19th-century work has almost always a regularity of finish which the original Greek or Etruscan pieces lack. It is almost true to say that some of these Victorian jewellers surpassed their masters in the fineness of their filigree goldwork, although they never quite equalled the delicacy of the Etruscans. The majority of the pieces, of course, were not made as direct imitations, but merely as a pastiche on antique modes. The use of gemstones unknown in classical times, or of coloured golds, is another easy method of identifying Victorian workmanship from the classic originals.

In necklaces, bracelets, and brooches, coloured golds such as red and green are often found, used in conjunction with fine granulated work. In addition, an attractive innovation of the period was the use of gold that had been bloomed. The bloom on gold—so popular in the late 19th century and a technique that might happily be revived —was achieved by dipping the metal into an acid solution. This faintly pitted the surface, and left the gold with a delicate matt appearance, which does, in fact, look not unlike the bloom on the skin of a peach.

Often found in conjunction with granulated gold-work and fine gold wire is the *millegrain* setting—so called because a number of tiny adjacent beads of metal are used to hold the gemstone in place. The combination of the innumerable minute fires of this type of setting with filigree and fanciful gold-work was something that had never before been achieved in jewellery. It is one of the unique products of the Victorian craftsman and deserves to be mentioned in the same breath with the work of the Renaissance goldsmith or of the 17th-century French enameller.

Quite commonly used in conjunction with delicate gold-work was the freshwater pearl—the product not of the oyster but of the pearl-bearing mussel (*Unio margaritiferus*). In Britain the streams of Scotland, particularly the Tay and the Spey, have long been famous for these pearls, and they were widely used in Victorian jewellery. Being small and delicate, the freshwater pearl accorded well with filigree gold settings. They were also often used to offset popular stones of the period, such as the topaz and the amethyst.

In Britain, as distinct from the Continent, another influence which made for the popularity of fine gold- and silver-work was that of India. The Indian jeweller for generations had been a master in the use of fine-drawn gold and silver wire, and in its application to bracelets, ear-rings, and necklaces. This Oriental work, brought or sent home by thousands of Victorian Anglo-Indians, undoubtedly contributed to the great filigree mode.

In the last decade of the 19th century the vogue for this filigree-work declined, as, with another inevitable swing of fashion's pendulum, the faceted gemstone came back to dominate the scene. The eclipse of the art of the *bijoutier* was also hastened by the influence of the Aesthetic Movement and by what was to be called in France *Art Nouveau*. At one end of the scale large dominant stones, enamelling, and an imitation of Renaissance work by designers like C. R.

Ashbee, set the new fashion. At the other end, the professional *joaillier* was establishing the modern trend by massing rows of faceted gemstones set in the new metal platinum.

The filigree gold-work and the Etruscan-style jewellery of the Victorian period is, without any doubt, one of the main achievements of the craftsman during the century. Not only are these pieces often impeccable in technique, they are also just as often aesthetically satisfying. In the final analysis one may agree with Sala in his summing up of the jewellery of his period:

'I do not see that it is possible to do anything in goldsmiths' work superior to what was done in Etruria in the inscrutable past; nor is it possible to give higher eulogy to, perhaps, the five best firms of goldsmiths in the world—Christofle, Froment-Meurice, Castellani, Hunt and Roskell, and Phillips—than to say that they have imitated the choicest productions of antiquity with consummate skill and complete success.'

4

Semi-precious Jewellery of the Nineteenth Century

'OURS is an age of transition; we are in the midst of the breaking up of the great deep of the past, and we are perhaps struggling after a wider and more distinct range of truth. We are, perhaps, labouring out great principles for the future; it may be that we are on the way to reconstruction after the deluge. But ours is certainly a chaotic period. The Exhibition shows that we are most skilful mimics—that we know how to reprint classics—that we can restore everything. But what do we create?'

Such was the somewhat gloomy comment of the *Morning Chronicle* leader-writer on the Great Exhibition of 1851. There was truth in his remarks as any student of the period will readily confess, but it is particularly interesting to note that even in 1851, at the nadir of Victorian taste, there were men with sufficient clear-sightedness and judgment to see that all was not well with Victorian design and craftsmanship.

Curiously enough, it was the craft of jewellery which suffered less from the deterioration of standards during the 19th century than any other. When the writer in the *Morning Chronicle* asked 'But what do we create?' he was thinking with despair, perhaps, of such monstrosities as the Kenilworth Buffet, of vulgar tea-sets, and of sentimental statuary. Victorian jeweller-craftsmen, on the other hand, created a vast wealth of finely executed and elegant pieces. There was vulgarity, of course, in many of the larger and more important diamond-set items, but in the realm of semi-

53

precious stone jewellery the ordinary working jeweller produced articles of which no age need feel ashamed.

The reason that jewellery was less affected by the Industrial Revolution than any other of the crafts was, as has been said, because jewellery in the precious metals could not be mechanized in the same way that, for instance, wood-working could be. Then, as today, a brooch or a pair of ear-clips, made in gold and set with precious or semi-precious stones, had to be worked, pierced, mounted, and set by hand. For so fine and precise a craft there is still no substitute for the trained human hand and eye.

The term 'semi-precious' needs some clarification. It does not refer to the 'costume' or fashion jewellery which is mass-produced and set with pastes or marcasites in gilded and plated base metals. A semi-precious stone is any gemstone which does not belong to the great quadrumvirate of the diamond, the ruby, the emerald, and the sapphire. It is only an artificial distinction of rarity, combined with high value, which sets these four stones apart from many others almost equally beautiful, such as the amethyst, the topaz, the peridot, and the garnet.

The shops of dealers in second-hand and antique jewellery still contain trays glistening with Victorian jewellery in gold and silver set with semi-precious stones. These pieces have survived because their intrinsic value was never high enough to warrant breaking them up and resetting them. The fact that they were never very expensive is no reason for despising them. The intelligent collector and student can still find some of the most exquisite examples of fine filigree gold-work, delicate mounting, and beautiful arrangements of stones among necklaces, brooches, and bracelets which are still—despite a steady rise in value—priced at under twenty-five pounds.

What was the reason for this proliferation of semi-precious jewellery during the Victorian era? There is no single answer to the question, but the main reason undoubtedly was the rise of a pros-

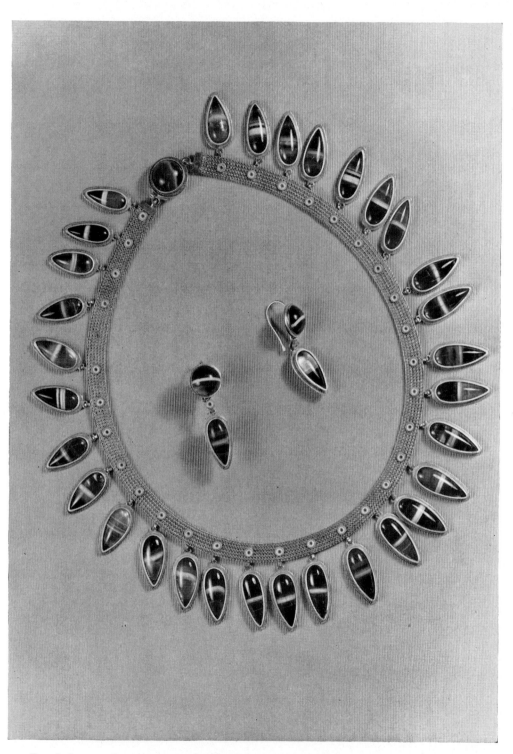

Banded agate drops in granulated settings with matching ear-rings. The small
rosettes on the necklace chain are enamelled gold.

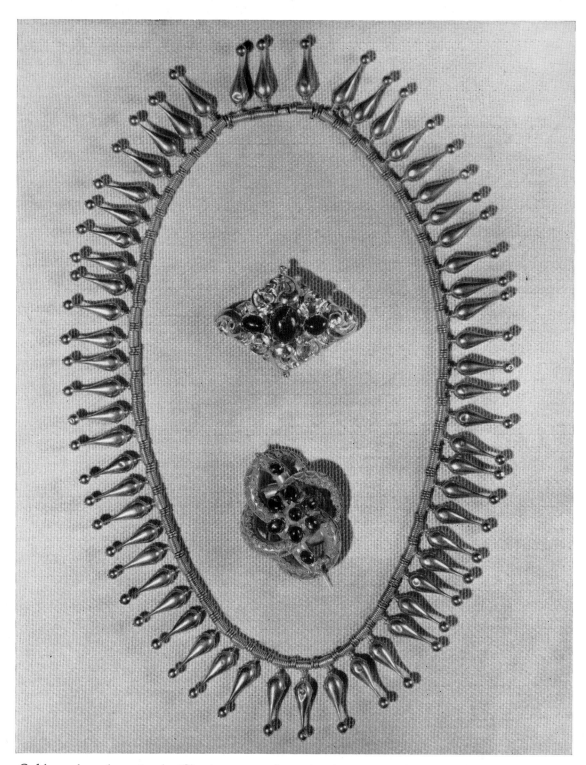

Gold pendant drops in the Classic manner form the decoration of this necklace. Gold scroll-work brooch set with *cabochon* garnets (*top*) and (*below*) another gold brooch set with garnets and decorated with granulation.

perous *bourgeoisie*, that large and powerful Victorian middle class who had money to spend and who copied the upper classes in their love of glitter and display. The middle-class Victorian wife could not, perhaps, emulate the diamonds and the pearls of the wealthy aristocracy, but there was no reason why she should not have amethysts and opals, or tourmalines and freshwater pearls. Such a class created an immense demand for semi-precious jewellery.

Another reason for the widespread use of these lesser gemstones was that England still looked to France for the lead in what was fashionable, and France—even after the Restoration—was a country where the aristocracy had suffered impoverishment. It was true that French fashions had reacted against the simplicity and the poverty of early 19th-century jewellery of the revolutionary period, but her court—although the Empress Eugénie attempted to revive some of the splendours of the past—could no longer afford the lavish display which had marked the courts of Louis XIV and Louis XV.

A third influence was exerted by the revived classicism of the period—a Neo-Classicism stemming largely from the discovery of Greco-Roman art forms at Herculaneum and Pompeii. The effect of these discoveries was to be found in the popularity of mosaic work, of cameos, and of intricate gold-work—all aspects of the jeweller's craft which called for great skill but not for the monumental massing of precious stones. Bright stones, however, and elegant gold-work were essential.

From 1870 onwards trade with South America formed a large part of the London and Parisian jeweller's business, and again the colour-loving Latins contributed towards the popularity of semi-precious stones. They preferred exotic displays and arrangements of colour to the somewhat cold classicism of the diamond. The discovery of the great opal mines in Australia gave yet another impetus—in England especially—towards the use of colourful stones in airy, delicate settings.

One of the most popular of all 19th-century stones was the

amethyst, birthstone for those born in February, with its colour range from deep purple down to pale lilac. The amethyst was particularly fashionable in the last quarter of the century. Often step- or trap-cut, with the facets lying in the long inclined planes that brought out its colour, the amethyst was an ideal stone for the *rivière* necklace. These *rivières*, which were fashionable for either day or evening wear, were necklaces composed of a row of large single stones, inconspicuously mounted, and depending for their attraction on the colour and quality of the stones. Important *rivières* were set with diamonds in silver or, towards the close of the century, in the new metal platinum. These have been broken up over the years, but semi-precious *rivières* set with amethysts or topaz still exist.

Peridot, alexandrite, tourmaline, spinel, and garnet were other colourful stones which were found particularly suitable for brooches and bracelets. The Victorians evolved some extremely fanciful brooches in which the play of coloured stones was well realized. Naturalistic designs of animals, birds, and insects were very popular from the 1860s onwards. A contemporary account of the designs and styles shown at the Paris Exhibition of 1867 gives one a picture of the prevailing taste for colour at that period:

'The harmonising of the colours was especially to be noticed. There were several imitations of birds, suitable either for brooches or for ornaments in the hair. The best was a peacock with spread tail, each eye in the feathers being set with an emerald. A small lyre bird from the same maker was also excellent. . . . There were some butterflies very nicely made and set, and I noticed several beetles as secret watches, the head being set with diamonds, the body a well-cut carbuncle (*cabochon*-garnet), the wings enamelled a nice bright amber colour.'

Beetles, butterflies, and birds provided exactly the type of motif in which these semi-precious stones could best be displayed. Small rose-cut diamonds were often used to give the pieces a sparkle, but the dominant feature was almost invariably the massing of lesser gemstones.

The opal, which has a colour range from a pale moony glow to jet black shot with fiery lights (the incomparable fire opal), was widely used in Victorian jewellery—sometimes to form the body of a bird or butterfly brooch, at others in matched series for necklaces and bracelets. It is curious that some people are still superstitious about this stone, for there appears to be no reason to account for its bad reputation. Indeed, even in fiction the first reference to an ill-omened opal is no earlier than the 19th century in Sir Walter Scott's novel, *Anne of Geierstein*. One true fact about the opal, which buyers of Victorian opal jewellery should be aware of, is that the stone is responsive to changes of temperature and is liable to expand and contract slightly. It is always wise to examine the settings of opal jewellery—and particularly claw settings—to see that the stone is firmly secured.

Unlike today, when a certain snobbishness has crept into the jewellery trade on the score of mixing the four 'precious' stones with the lesser gemstones, the Victorian craftsman had no feeling that there was a kind of 'Royal Enclosure' which could only be entered by the diamond, the ruby, the sapphire, and the emerald. In the *Official Description and Illustrated Catalogue of the Great Exhibition, 1851* (Vol. II), we find all the pieces of the exhibiting jewellers listed. It is interesting to note that 'Garrard, R. and S., and Co., Panton Street, Haymarket, Goldsmiths to the Queen', thought nothing of mixing opals with brilliant-cut diamonds or the 'jacinth' (zircon) with emeralds and rubies. The following extract from the jewellery displayed by Garrard and Co. gives an idea of this happy Victorian habit of offsetting lesser with precious gemstones—a habit which was to increase as the century advanced:

Suite of very fine opals and brilliants, consisting of necklace and stomacher, ear-rings, bracelet, and pin.

Bracelet with natural pink topaz, set with brilliants and enamelled.

Bracelet in coloured gold, with large carbuncle and brilliant centre.

Pendant of opals, rubies, and brilliants, and solid opal drop.

Fly brooches of emerald, sapphire, opals, and brilliants; of pearl, sapphire, tourmaline, and brilliants; of jacinth, emerald, ruby, and brilliants.

Rock crystal was quite often used by the Victorian jeweller, and a favourite was the rock-crystal heart designed to be hung as a pendant on a length of velvet ribbon. One of the noblest of the diamond substitutes, rock crystal should never be confused with paste. The word 'rhinestone' often nowadays applied to paste is a complete misnomer. The true 'rhinestone' is a kind of colourless quartz often used during the 19th century in the same way as crystal.

The Victorian jeweller ransacked the earth's Aladdin's cave to find colourful stones. Garnets, whether faceted or cut *en cabochon* (the so-called carbuncle) were among the principal favourites, and the rich, port-wine red of massed garnets on a pendant or necklace often achieves an effect which more expensive stones fail to do.

A brief account of the principal coloured stones used by the Victorian jeweller, and the uses to which they were put, may be of help to the student and collector.

Agate. This is a term applied to concentrically banded pieces of onyx (quartz) often used for brooches. The agate was commonly used in the popular Scottish jewellery of the period. It was usually dyed before being set in a piece of jewellery.

Alexandrite. This is one of the chrysoberyl family and was named after the Tsar, Alexander II. Found in Russia and Ceylon, the stone is remarkably dichroic (exhibiting different colours according to the direction from which it is viewed, and whether seen in natural or artificial light).

Leaves and foliage were popular motifs during the mid-Victorian period. An amethyst and gilt necklace.

The enamelled brooch is set with diamonds, rubies, and pearls, in the 'Holbein' or 'Tudor' style. The three rings are good examples of the excellence of much Victorian workmanship. (*Left*) Amethyst and pearl cluster ring. (*Centre*) Star sapphire. (*Right*) Turquoise and pearl cluster with finely modelled shoulders.

A good example of saw-piercing, filigree, and engraved work. Gold, set with good-quality amethyst.

(*Above, left*) A pearl and diamond gold brooch in the Neo-Classic manner. (*Above, right*) Finely enamelled pendant brooch in the 'Holbein' style set with chrysoberyls and a carbuncle in the centre. Below, onyx, diamond, and gold 'padlock' brooch. The central device surmounted by the dolphin lifts to disclose a place for a lock of hair.

Amethysts set in a formal gold cartouche.

Amber. The fossilized resins of prehistoric trees, it was widely used in necklaces, rings, and bracelets. An attractive orange-coloured amber which comes from Sicily was popular during this period.

Amethyst. Found in Russia, Brazil, and Uruguay, as well as Ceylon, it was a great favourite, set in gold, for necklaces and bracelets.

Aquamarine. An attractive pale blue stone of the beryl family. Step- or trap-cut, it was popular in the 19th century, particularly the greenish variety.

Bloodstone. Used commonly for signet-rings, a dark green chalcedony interspersed with drops of red.

Cat's Eye. A term commonly used for the *cabochon*-cut chrysoberyl and derived from the attractive line of lights which shift across the stone. The Cat's Eye is usually found mounted in a ring.

Coral. The skeleton of the coral polyp. The widespread use of this material during the Early Victorian period led to a subsequent fall in favour, although it was still employed for ear-rings and small necklaces until the close of the century. Most of the coral used in English jewellery came from the Mediterranean.

Cornelian. Another member of the chalcedony family, of a reddish colour and used for seals and beads.

Garnet. Its uses are described above. It was sometimes in the Victorian period called the 'Cape Ruby'. A demantoid garnet is green, as opposed to the better-known almandine or pyrope garnets, which are both deep red.

Jade. Popular in Victorian and Edwardian times for ear-rings and rings. The best, of clear green colour, was also used for necklaces.

Jasper. The name given to a type of chalcedony, strongly marked with reds, greens, and browns. Found in brooches and sometimes bracelets.

Lapis Lazuli. This fascinating deep blue stone, a favourite with the early Egyptian jewellers, had a revival of popularity during the 19th century. An artificially coloured hornstone or jasper was also used by the Victorians, but is easily detectable from lapis lazuli because it does not contain the gold-coloured specks of iron pyrites which are half the fascination of the true stone.

Onyx. Together with agate, a kind of quartz marked by bands of light and dark colours. Mainly found in brooches and bracelets.

Opals. Usually cut as flat *cabochons*, they played an important part in Victorian jewellery (see above).

Peridot or **Olivine.** Under either name it is a distinctive yellowish or bottle-green stone, and is quite commonly found in Victorian brooches and pendants.

Sard. Similar to cornelian and used for seals—the name *sard* is applied to the stone when it is a russet-red colour.

Sardonyx. A portmanteau word for sard and onyx, denoting an onyx with red or russet banding.

Spinel. With a range of colour from red through yellow to blue, it was often used for rings. When red, the spinel is popularly miscalled a balas ruby.

Topaz. Often used in necklaces and bracelets, it is, when well matched, one of the loveliest of the lesser gemstones in Victorian jewellery. Apart from the rich sherry-brown, the topaz can also be blue, colourless, or pink.

Tourmaline. Another stone with a wide colour range—green or red usually, and sometimes combining the two colours in one stone.

Turquoise. Usually cut *en cabochon*, its attractive blue colour made it popular for large bracelets and brooches.

Zircon. As found in Victorian jewellery, it is generally in its natural brown state. The colourless or blue zircon (the product of heat treatment) is only occasionally found at this period, as the Ceylonese technique for changing its colour was hardly known.

This brief outline of the principal coloured stones used by the Victorian jeweller gives an indication of the wide palette which he had at his disposal. Never before—or since—have they been so skilfully or widely used. There are still a few London and Paris firms which specialize in coloured gemstone brooches and clips, but nowadays these are nearly all destined for the South American market. Except in Latin America, it would seem that the modern woman, if she cannot afford jewellery set with the major stones, prefers the purely artificial colour of pastes.

The amateur of gems and jewellery can be guided in collecting this semi-precious stone jewellery only by his own good taste. One thing always to remember is that the finer quality the setting so, almost invariably, the finer quality are the stones. The Victorians lavished some of their most exquisite filigree gold-work on stones like the topaz and the amethyst—work that has a degree of delicacy almost without rival in the history of jewellery.

5

Popular Jewellery: its Ancestry and its Development in the Nineteenth Century

DURING the Victorian period mass-production of the cheaper ranges of jewellery became established. For the first time in history all classes of the population were able to buy luxury articles. In a review of the *Gilt Toy Trade* made in 1868, the writer makes the following statement: 'There is no valid reason why the factory girl should not display her gilt buckle and brooch of the same design as the golden one worn by the lady of the villa. Art may thus serve the community by cheapening the cost of the beautiful, and affording gratification to the humblest members of society, by superior designs reproduced in the cheapest possible form, and attainable by all.'

Allowing for the complacent tone (a feature of Victorian journalism of the time) there is some truth in the writer's statement. Although the mass-production of certain articles had already begun by the late 18th century, it was not until the Victorian era that machinery was sufficiently advanced to cater for the demands of an ever-increasing population.

The basis of all popular or costume jewellery is the imitation gemstone, and the history of these 'pseudo-gems' is almost as old as the history of genuine stones. Today, when both diamonds and rubies can be manufactured in the laboratory, it is difficult to realize that this is the culmination of centuries of striving by jewellers, alchemists, and glass-craftsmen. To produce or simulate the fire of true

66

Turquoise and pearl suite. A good example of the filigree and granulated style.

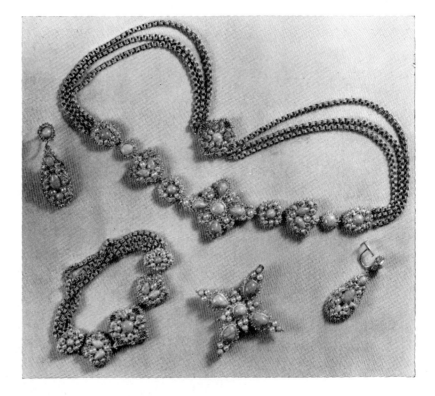

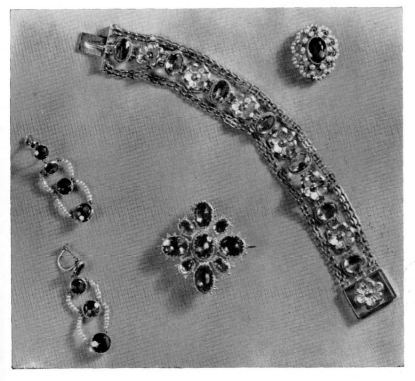

(*Top*) Amethyst and pearl brooch in filigree setting; topaz and gold floral bracelet. (*Centre*) Amethyst brooch in delicate granulated setting. (*Left*) Pearl and amethyst pendant ear-rings.

Ear piercing. A contemporary print, after E. R. Cooper.

gemstones has been one of mankind's dreams since the dawn of civilization.

It is curious to reflect that, rather in the manner of the 19th-century European buying the friendship of African tribes with glass beads, so the Roman once astonished the Ancient Briton with the splendour of paste necklaces and bracelets. Even before the Romans had landed in England, Phoenician traders were bargaining on the Cornish coast for tin and hides with the aid of green, dark blue, and white paste stones. It is more than likely that the first 'civilized' piece of jewellery ever worn in the British Isles was made of paste. Paste, in fact, has as long a history in Europe as almost any true gemstone. Its popularity has only twice been rivalled—and then for only a comparatively brief period—by marcasite and cut-steel.

Paste jewellery has been found on the sites of the very earliest civilizations, but the greatest paste-makers of the ancient world were the Egyptians, among whom paste was reckoned on a basis of almost complete equality with the true gemstone. One of the earliest references to paste—and one which may divert the modern woman as she clips on her paste-set ear-rings—is in Herodotus, where he refers to the pendant paste ear-rings with which the Egyptians adorned the ears of their sacred crocodiles! 'Melted stone', Herodotus calls its; no bad description for what is basically no more than high-grade glass.

The earliest paste necklaces which have been found in Western Europe were most probably of Egyptian manufacture, for the Phoenicians were essentially the 'middle-men' and not the producers of the ancient world. Pastes similar to those found in France and Britain have also been discovered in Mediterranean islands such as Sardinia and Ibiza, two other 'markets' of the Phoenician trader.

That the composition of paste has changed little over the centuries can be seen by a comparison between an analysis of an Egyptian blue paste and an analysis of a paste made to the famous formula of Strass. The Egyptian has:

	per cent
Silica	71·0
Red lead	14·0
Copper oxide	12·5
Alumina	1·0
Lime	1·5

Strass's formula has:

	parts
Silica	100·0
Red lead	135·0
Potash	53·1
Calcined borax	6·8

As can be seen, the principal difference here is the considerably higher percentage of lead used by Strass in his paste. This was his great discovery. The high proportion of lead gave the paste exactly that lustre and clarity which was required at the time for producing the diamond 'imitation'. This is the type of paste with which the collector will be familiar.

Even after the withdrawal of the Romans, the art of paste-making was preserved in Western Europe. It survived the Middle Ages, and many of the well-known mediaeval pieces in museums contain paste stones. It is more than likely that, could they all be analysed, it would be found that many more 'stones' are paste than has ever been suspected.

But the paste which interests the collector is that which dates from the 18th century. The techniques of making these pastes, and the pieces of jewellery in which they were set, have often been reviewed. In view of their later popularity, it is perhaps worth inquiring why the 18th century in England witnessed such a revival of an old art. There are two basic reasons, one sociological and the other technical.

Popular Jewellery

For the first time in the history of Europe there evolved during the 18th century a large and prosperous middle class in England. This class was something quite new in the history of European society. It was true that there had often before been a prosperous merchant class (even in Imperial Rome there had been a wealthy 'Freedman' section of society), but never in any country had a whole large section of a nation been in the position to live as comfortably, and almost as extravagantly, as the ruling class.

This new middle class created inevitably a new condition of demand and supply. No longer content like the earlier money-lender or merchant to remain, despite their wealth, within the bounds of fashion and dress decreed them from above, the English middle class had educated tastes as well as money to spend. It is worth reflecting that for every large, world-famous Georgian country house there are a dozen or so small houses in the nearest village of almost equal quality, built for local merchants and tradesmen. In the miniature sphere of jewellery the situation was very similar.

If the courtier or his lady would have

> *A sapphire bodkin for the hair*
> *Or sparkling facet diamonds there,*

then his tradesman, if he could not afford diamonds, would at least have paste, and good paste at that. Again, just as in the question of houses, the costume-jewellery brooch or shoe buckle was hardly less elegant than the authentic article.

It is often stated that it was the great improvement in glass-making techniques during this century which led to the production of so many fine paste-set pieces, but this is putting the cart before the horse. The real reason was the change in gem-set jewellery fashions; the change which made the 18th century the age of the diamond and the faceted stone. It was the improvement in gem-cutting techniques which led to the gemstone being accorded pride of place in this century's jewellery rather than, as before, the mount and the setting. Without the discovery of the brilliant cut, and without the general improvement in lapidary work, there would have been no call for the glass-maker to turn his attention to the manufacture of paste. It was the overriding popularity of the diamond and the faceted gemstone that created the demand for a popular substitute and imitation. If this was true of the 18th century, it was equally true of its successor.

Once the demand existed, the ingenuity of the glass-maker was ready to meet it. The discoveries of Strass on the Continent and of Ravenscroft in England were paralleled by many humbler glass-makers whose names have gone unrecorded. The 'soft smoky hue' of this 18th-century diamond paste is often praised—sometimes for the wrong reasons. It is not, as has occasionally been stated, due to some secret of the paste-maker. (We know and can imitate his formula.) It is the result of time not of art, for these pastes have lost some of their polish over the years and have been further discoloured by the sulphur in the smoke of modern cities. Many pastes also, particularly those set in *pavé* or rub-over settings, were backed with foils to enhance their brilliance, and these foils have also become discoloured.

Although the prosperity of the middle classes and the desire to imitate the fashionable diamond were the principal factors behind the manufacture of this 18th-century costume jewellery, a further impetus was derived from an unlikely source. This was the prevalence of highwaymen and cut-purses upon the roads.

A journey between one town and another was not without its hazards. Numerous accounts tell of the theft of personal jewellery from coach travellers. The wise man and woman, therefore, left their valuables at home and travelled as lightly as was possible. Still, the fact remained that it was a decorative age, and many of the travellers would be on their way to and from towns and entertainments where jewellery was a necessity. It was here that paste played its part. Ear-rings, shoe buckles, necklaces, bracelets—all could be attractively 'counterfeited'. Their loss would be small compared with the loss of diamonds.

Marcasite jewellery also became fashionable during this century, and continued in favour throughout the Victorian period. The term 'marcasite' is, in fact, a misnomer, for the mineral used by jewellers for 'marcasites' is iron pyrites and not marcasite. The word is also sometimes spelled 'marquisite', the derivation here most probably coming from marquise rings in which marcasites were often set. The mineral, then as now, was faceted by hand and a traditional industry still exists in France for the cutting and faceting of the stone.

Although, by its very nature, marcasite could never be a diamond substitute, it had its own particular qualities—qualities which made it especially effective as a surround or frame for coloured stones and enamels. Marcasite, like paste, was usually set in silver, although pewter is not unknown as a setting, particularly in shoe buckles. The marcasite stones, being very small, were usually set in long ribbon-like bands—the glitter and sparkle coming *off* the hard, faceted surface, as opposed to paste and real stones where the brilliance is caused by the reflected play of light *through* the stone.

The marcasites found in 18th- and 19th-century pieces are normally rose cut and are *pavé*-set, the turned-over edges of the retaining metal adding to their sparkle. Marcasite was essentially a French importation and became popular only because England looked to Paris for her fashions. In France it was the economic stringencies of Louis XV's Minister of Finance, M. de Silhouette, that led to the widespread adoption of marcasite by the French court. Like the paper portraits which still bear his name and which were derisively termed 'Silhouettes' to mark their cheapness, marcasite was the offspring of an economy wave.

The third glittering 'diamond substitute', cut-steel, is less well known but still of considerable interest. In April, 1771, when the articles of the Birmingham Metal Company were signed by the

'Joint traders in the Trade, Art and Mystery of making and selling Brass, Spelter and other metals', a great industry was born and the foundations of a major industrial city was laid. What is less well known is that a principal source of Birmingham's revenue in those early days was the manufacture of cut-steel jewellery. Extremely popular throughout the latter half of the 18th century, cut-steel jewellery is rather similar to marcasite in appearance. The cut-steel 'heads' are of approximately the same size as marcasites and, like the natural stone, were individually faceted (usually by cheap female labour). They were then polished and set in their mounts, individually again, being held in place with small steel rivets. The work involved was considerable. A cut-steel buckle has probably quite as many hours involved in its fabrication as a buckle of paste or marcasite. (These in themselves, if well set, entail nearly as much handwork and skill as if they were diamonds.)

Cut-steel heads were used, again like marcasites, in ribbon-like designs and were particularly suitable for framing cameos and enamels. The manufacture of cut-steel jewellery became so important to Birmingham that, when the fashion for shoe-buckles showed signs of declining, the manufacturers appealed to the Prince Regent to give the public a lead by wearing buckles of cut-steel. The Regent's influence in fashion, however, was less than the manufacturers—or perhaps even he—suspected, and the demand for them continued to decline. They would have done better, perhaps, if they had appealed to a more decisive *arbiter elegantiarum*, such as 'Beau' Brummell.

Throughout the 19th century cut-steel was still used in popular jewellery, although less and less for articles of any quality. The development of die-stamping, apart from bringing into being a whole class of cheap gilt jewellery which had been unknown before, was now applied to cut-steel. Instead of each steel head being individually made and hand set, long ribbons of steel were now impressed with 'pseudo-heads'. These ribbons could be bought wholesale by the manufacturing jeweller, who had little more to do when making the surround for, say, a locket than to cut the steel ribbon at a given point and solder it into place. The cut-steel jewellery which still survives from the Victorian period can easily be detected from its 18th-century progenitor. It is invariably coarse and cheap in appearance, and a swift inspection will reveal that the cut-steel heads are not separately made and riveted, but that they are only impressed on to a long ribbon of metal. With the expansion of the cheap paste-making manufactories, and the growing popularity of gilded base-metal jewellery, even the imitation cut-steel border lost its appeal.

Cut-steel jewellery is no longer made today, although its older ancestor, paste, is still as popular as ever. Even marcasites, despite some decline in popularity, are still being used in modern jewellery. But modern paste- and marcasite-set pieces bear little relation to the articles of genuine craftsmanship from which they are descended. Only too often they are crudely held in 'open' settings with jeweller's cement, instead of being individually hand-set as they were in the past.

An analysis of the Birmingham and cheap jewellery trade published in the 1860s provides one with an interesting picture of the change which had taken place between the Georgian period and the Victorian.

'At the commencement of the present century,' the review begins, 'it is probable that some four hundred artisans were employed in ten or twelve manufactories: those working in gold made principally seals, keys, and watch chains, whilst the silver workers produced shoe, knee, and other buckles, as well as considerable quantities of comb ornaments set with conspicuous paste or imitation stones.

'The chief seat of trade formerly was Derby, where large quantities of common and medium jewellery were produced, Edinburgh and London manufacturing the finest goods. The trade has almost disappeared from the former places, and London now depends mainly upon Birmingham for the supply of articles suitable for the middle classes. Since 1836 the trade may be said to have been in a flourishing condition, but during the last twenty years its progress has been almost marvellous. . . . With the exception of a few machinists (and in very busy seasons the workmen in the gun trade), the jewellers are the best paid of the Birmingham artisans. The rate, of course, varies considerably, but he is a poor workman who can only earn 25s. weekly; 30s. to 50s. may be considered the average of wages. Enamellers frequently gain as much as from £3 to £5 weekly. Boys are usually apprenticed at fourteen, when they earn 4s. per week, which is increased annually until they are twenty-one, when they generally receive 10s. or 11s., working as a rule from eight to seven, with intervals of an hour and a quarter for dinner, and half an hour for tea. Youths sometimes make a considerable sum working overtime.

'There are comparatively few manufactories, most of the articles for which it is noted being produced in shops where five to fifty hands are employed. Probably one out of every ten of the master jewellers, who are now carrying on business on their own account, were originally workmen. In one instance, at least, not less than twelve independent concerns are now in active operation, each employing a number of hands; the principals of these twelve concerns having all been employed as apprentices or workmen in a manufactory which itself has been established within twenty-five years.

'All that is needed for a workman to start as a master is a peculiarly-shaped bench and a leather apron, one or two pounds' worth of tools (including a large blow pipe) and for material, a few sovereigns, and some ounces of copper and zinc. His shop may be the top-room of his house, or a small building over the wash-house, at a rent of 2s. or 2s. 6d. per week, and the indispensable gas jet, which the gas company will supply on credit. With these appliances, and a

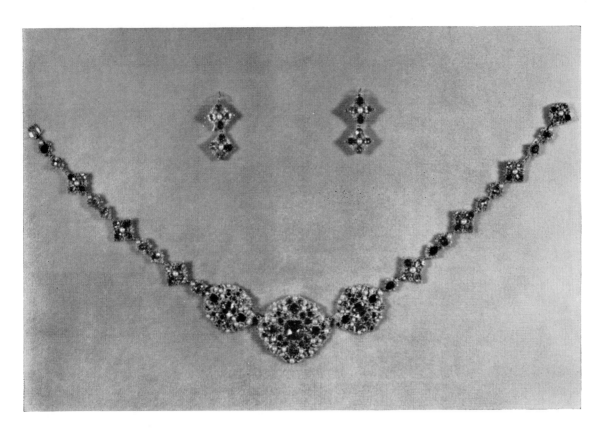

Necklace and ear-rings in gold
set with emeralds, rubies, and
pearls. Early Victorian.

Two necklaces with ear-rings *en
suite*: (*top*) gold set with pearls;
(*below*) carved amethysts in gold
setting.

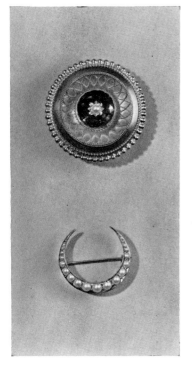

(*Above*) Gold brooch set with emeralds, diamonds, and rubies. Necklace and ear-rings in gold with peridots in diamond surrounds.

(*Extreme left*) Pearl, amethyst, and gold brooch in a classic design. Pearl crescent brooch, below.
(*Left*) Top, amethyst and pearl brooch. Below, pearl and diamond brooch in gold.

skilful hand, he may produce scarf-pins, studs, links, rings, lockets, etc., for all of which he will find a ready market on the Saturday among the numerous "factors" whose special business it is to supply the shopkeepers throughout the country.'

Although, as the century advanced, such small firms tended more and more to become amalgamated into expanding and success-ful rivals, such was essentially the pattern of the Birmingham and London cheap jewellery industry during this period. A revealing comment on the transference of ideas and patterns occurs later on in the same report:

'Many ideas may have been gathered from France and Italy, yet it will be found that the manufacturers of jewellery are not copyists, and though they may study the character and style of ancient and modern workers, yet they design and invent in the main for them-selves, and their productions have acquired a reputation which rivals that possessed by Paris or Rome.

'It is well known that the agents of the German manufacturers continually transmit to their principals the newest patterns which Birmingham produces. These are copied to a considerable extent in Frankfurt, Hanau, and other towns, and afterwards enter into com-petition with the original articles in foreign, colonial, and sometimes in the home markets too.'

Such a comment is revealing. It foreshadows that trade rivalry which was finally to lead to the destruction of the comfortable Victorian and Edwardian world. It should also remind collectors, students, and dealers, who may be too prone to ascribe the origin of a piece of jewellery confidently to one country or another, that such certainty is well-nigh impossible. What was true of the cheap jewel-lery market was no less true of precious jewellery.

The shops of antique dealers, and even—regrettably—the display cabinets of museums, are often too confident with their objects labelled 'English. 1850' or 'French. Late 1870s'. Unless the exact history of a piece of jewellery is known, it is rarely possible to ascribe its date and provenance with complete certainty. Even in popular jewellery, of course, there are certain recognizable signs which may indicate whether the piece was made in England or France, Italy or Germany; even so, as the century advanced the internationalism which had been a feature of jewellery ever since the publication of pattern books in the 16th century became more and more marked.

The use of pinchbeck, which had played so large a part in the cheaper jewellery of the late 18th century, declined rapidly after the invention of electro-gilding. This process of plating a die-stamped piece of base metal so as to give it a pseudo-gold or silver colour was one of the chief technical advances of the 19th century.

'Gilt Toys', to quote from a reviewer of jewellery fashion in the 1870s, 'is a technical term embracing personal ornaments of all descriptions in which metals, gilt, or simply coloured, are used either alone or in combination with imitation or real stones, cameos, mosaics, ivory, bone, jet, and other materials. The trade is largely carried on in Birmingham, and has displayed, to a considerable extent, articles of a similar kind which were imported from France or Germany. The beauty of many of these articles, both as regards form and finish, is surprising. The process of electro-gilding, to which the development of the trade is principally owing, enables the manufacturer to produce a surface that is frequently indistinguishable from the finest gold-work.

'The fine Etruscan style, which is now so current in gold-work, is imitated in a die, and stamped up to bear a close resemblance. The beautiful hinges and snaps, made by the goldsmith with the most delicate tools, are effectually imitated by bending, or making an indentation, by a screw press, in a simple piece of metal.'

A surprising number of these cheap articles have survived, even taking into consideration the fact that they were made in their thousands. One of the reasons for this is that the Victorian jeweller tended to make these 'gilt toys' of heavier metal and with a heavier electro-deposit than would nowadays be considered economical.

The heavy materials used by the dressmaker of the time, combined with a love of solid and substantial articles, meant that even a pierced gilt brooch was made to last. Its modern successor is designed, like the modern car, to have a short life and to be discarded at the end of a year or two for the creations of the next year.

Between the cheapest grade of gilt jewellery and the ornaments made of gold there lay an intermediate category—plated jewellery. This was of the type which today would be described as 'rolled gold'. It was far more widely used for jewellery in Victorian days than is the case today. Pieces of what we would term 'costume jewellery' were more timeless then than now.

In the 20th century, when the great fashion houses of Paris decree a new 'line', it is customary for the manufacturers of costume jewellery to change their styling to accord with the new clothes. For instance, with the advent of the 'New Look' in recent post-war years a great range of costume jewellery was produced that captured something of the Victorian or Edwardian flavour of the clothes. Eight years later, when the styles of the 1920s were being revived, the manufacturer of costume jewellery was making bead necklaces and bracelets, long necklaces of imitation pearls, and simple pendant ear-rings. In Victorian days, however, dress fashions did not change so often nor so conclusively, and a piece of cheap jewellery was expected to last for a good number of years. It was this aspect of fashion which made 'rolled' gold or silver jewellery more extensively used then than now. The peculiarity of this type of jewellery consists in the application, by fusion, of thin plates of gold or silver on to thicker plates of common metal. The technique was used for bracelets, lockets, pendants, and many of the commoner items of jewellery.

The standard of English gilt and rolled-gold jewellery was very high, and its finish was usually better than that of the Continent. James Pamplin, a working jeweller of Birmingham, remarked about the exhibits at the Paris International Exhibition of 1867 that: 'The English work of this description is superior in colour [to the Continental], being less brassy than the work of other nations. It is inferior to the French design, and to that nation only, but superior in finish.'

This superiority of finish is something that distinguishes English from Continental jewellery throughout the century. The French, as Pamplin noted, were invariably better designers than the English, but aimed only at a pleasing appearance and held to the maxim that 'What the eye does not see the heart does not grieve about'. In cheaper items of jewellery it was only the methodical Germans who competed with the English in the finish of their pieces. Throughout the centuries, whether the jewellery in question is of the highest quality or merely a 'gilt toy', the hall-mark of an English piece is the quality of its craftsmanship and its finish. The hinges of pins, the backs of ear-rings, the unseen corners and interiors of lockets and cases were always regarded by the English jeweller as meriting as much attention as the openly displayed sections. Such an outlook is a question of temperament, but it can often assist in determining whether a piece was made by an English or German craftsman, or by a Latin—for whom the immediate surface appeal was all that counted.

The imitation pearl, so predominant a feature of the last twenty years in European jewellery, was not unknown to the Victorians. Imitation pearls, in fact, were being made as early as the 16th century, when the French jeweller, Jacquin, was given a monopoly for them by Henri IV. Owing to their fragile nature, few of the imitation pearls made in the 19th century have survived. Unlike the modern imitation pearl, which has a solid core (of glass or plastic), the 19th-century imitation was a hollow glass sphere, extremely thin, and coated inside with what was called 'Oriental essence'. This 'essence' was made from a precipitate of the scales of a small silvery fish, the bleak (*Alburnus lucidus*). The inside of the glass was lightly coated with this silvery deposit, and the sphere was then filled up

(*Right*) Gold and turquoise bracelet.

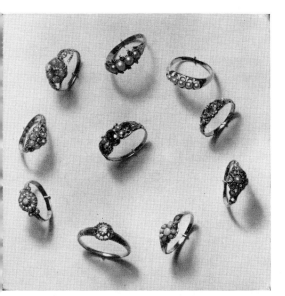

(*Left*) A cluster of Victorian rings. Pearls, turquoise, diamonds, and amethysts are used in the settings. Sawpiercing and engraving of the shoulders of the rings was a common feature of the period.

(*Right*) The minuterie of the era: stick pins, small brooches, and gold chain purse. Even on such comparatively unimportant pieces the work was usually good. The enamelling of the round pin-brooch, left centre, is a case in point.

83

An early amethyst necklace set
in gold. The pendant is an
addition.

Among lesser gemstones the garnet
remained one of the most fashionable
stones. A brilliant-cut almandine garnet
star pendant.

84

with white wax. The 19th-century imitation pearls are not as good facsimiles as the modern ones, but have a certain charm of their own. They are rarely found in England, where they did not enjoy as great a vogue as on the Continent.

In Early Victorian jewellery the mosaic was very fashionable. The enthusiasm for this style of work stemmed from the discoveries at Herculaneum and Pompeii, and was part of the Neo-Classical or Greek revival that influenced not only the furniture and metal-work of the period but even the dress fashions.

Both Rome and Paris were engaged in the production of mosaic-work and, although there is no doubt that some English jewellers emulated them, the majority of mosaics undoubtedly came from the Continent. Some of the better class hard-stone (*pietre dure*) work of the Roman jewellers was extremely attractive, capturing in minia-ture the colour and the vitality of the classic originals. In England such mosaics were often set as brooches, sometimes in bracelets and sometimes even in necklaces. The fashion was fleetingly revived by Castellani and his imitators but, generally speaking, the mosaic be-longs to the period prior to 1851. By 1865 a commentator on jewel-lery fashion could write: 'Formerly mosaics produced in Rome were largely used [by English jewellers], but are now out of fashion. Shell cameos, however, are still in regular but not large demand. A better class of stone cameo is used in considerable quantities, these being fifteen to twenty times the value of shell cameos.'

Shell cameos had begun to be popular in the 18th century and coincided with the Classical Revival. In England they were to some extent superseded by the cameos of Wedgwood and the glass cameos of the Scots craftsman, Tassie. In the 1840s and 1850s they had a revival of popularity, and continued to be made up into brooches, necklaces, and bracelets until the 1914-18 war.

These mollusc-shell cameos were imported in bulk from Italy and were mounted and set in London and Birmingham. The cheaper and less expensive were mounted in gilded or rolled-gold frames, and the better quality in gold. This type of cameo is carved out of the comparatively soft mollusc shell with hand tools similar to those used in silver chasing and engraving. It does not need to be worked upon the wheel like the true, hard-stone cameo. So many thousands of Victorian cameos are still in existence that it is almost impossible to give the student any indications as to what distinguishes a good shell cameo from a poor one. The quality of the carving is something that can, of course, be easily recognized by the trained eye, as well as the quality of the setting. It stands to reason that the finer examples were set in gold, often very elaborately. Some of these shell cameos are small masterpieces of carving extremely attractive in their own right. The coarser examples, which have been mass-produced in Italy for over a hundred years, can easily be detected from the finely worked pieces that came from Roman jewellers of quality.

The collector should be warned against a type of imitation cameo which has come on the market within recent years, and which is an imitation of a shell cameo made by injection-moulding in plastics. These can swiftly be detected by comparison with a real shell cameo. The settings are coarse, gilded base-metals, and the plastic surface has a completely different 'feel' to the mollusc shell. These modern copies are marketed as costume jewellery, but they do occasionally fall into the hands of dealers in second-hand jewellery who are sufficiently ignorant as to try to sell them as Victorian mollusc cameos.

An examination of the *Official Catalogue of the Great Exhibition, 1851* reveals that the vogue for Scottish jewellery had already become apparent. The predilection of both Queen Victoria and her Consort for the Scottish Highlands and the newly acquired royal residence at Balmoral, purchased in 1852, played an important part in shaping Victorian tastes. The influence of the Romantic writers, and especially Sir Walter Scott, on the Victorian public made itself felt in an idealization of the romantic Celt. The growing industrial-

ization of England and the ugliness with which the Industrial
Revolution surrounded the average Victorian made him prone to
dreams of a simple, open-air life among the heather and the moun-
tains. The jeweller was not slow to see the possibilities of this romantic Scottish jewellery, and it was not only in Scotland itself that
the taste for enamelled tartan motifs, cairngorms in silver settings,
and rams' heads as snuff-boxes was indulged.

This revival of Scottish jewellery is a predominantly Victorian
feature; interest in it had been confined to north of the border in
previous centuries, and today it is largely the expatriate Scot or
people of Scottish descent in the Commonwealth overseas who in-
dulge this taste for the jewellery of their ancestors. During the 19th
century, however, the vogue for all things Scottish affected the
whole of England. Even those with no pretence to Highland blood
wore cairngorm brooches, grouse feet mounted in silver, or set a
ram's head on their sideboards or a copy of Landseer's 'Monarch of
the Glen' in the entrance hall.

Typical products of this Scottish revival are recorded in the
Catalogue of the Great Exhibition:

Marshall & Sons, 87, Great George Street, Edinburgh.
Set of accoutrements for a Highland dress, with chased silver
mountings studded with carbuncles and cairngorms, viz. goat-
skin purse, broad sword, dirk, powder horn, skean dhu, or hunt-
ing knife; plaid brooch; sword-belt, body-belt; shoe buckles;
pistols; Athol bonnet; stag's head.
Walter Baird, 7, Argyle Street, Glasgow.
A Scotch ram's head, each horn measuring 3 feet 5 inches,
mounted as a snuff-box and cigar-case, in gold and silver, adorned
with a cairngorm and Scotch amethyst stones.
M. M'Gregor, Perth.
Ram's head, mounted in silver, with Scotch stones, as a snuff-
box and cigar-case.

Meyer & Mortimer, George Street, Edinburgh.

Ornaments of different Highland regiments in Her Majesty's service. Also, patterns of the tartans and kilts, with specimens of dirks, purses, brooches, and other accoutrements worn by each.

One of the consequences of this enthusiasm was a revival of interest in the freshwater pearl. Although the freshwater pearl should strictly be classified under precious jewellery, its use was so widespread during the 19th century that it seems to demand inclusion under the term 'Popular'. The product not of the oyster but of the pearl mussel (*Unio margaritiferus*), the freshwater pearl is common to the waters of the Tay and the Spey. For centuries it had been used in Scottish jewellery, but during the Victorian period it was widely employed for surrounds to brooches and lockets and for ear-rings. These delicate small pearls can be seen at their best in conjunction with filigree gold mounts, where their delicacy and soft sheen help to offset the colours of semi-precious stones.

In Early Victorian jewellery coral figured as one of the most popular materials. So fashionable was it that, when coral finally went out of favour, it went out completely. The English market was flooded with coral carvings of every description up to and including the year of the Great Exhibition.

A typical display of coral jewellery was the following:

Paravagua & Casella, of Brabant Court, Philpot Lane.

Carving representing Bacchus, of the finest coral, with pedestal and fittings. Gigantic child's coral. Coral bracelet, set in gold. Necklace of diamond-cut coral. Pair of coral drops. Coral cameos. Diamond-cut coral pieces.

Some of this Early Victorian coral work can be very fine and well carved, particularly the better-quality cameos. The settings, however, tend to be rather too heavy for the modern taste, and coral has never regained its popularity, although it did experience a brief

A typical coral suite of the type fashionable in the mid-century. The granulated settings are well executed.

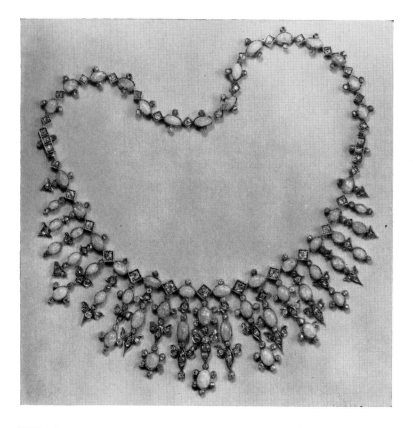

(*Left*) A fine opal and diamond necklace, the opals carefully selected for colour.

(*Below*) Garnet bracelet and a typical *cabochon* garnet brooch, the central stone surrounded by brilliant-cut garnets.

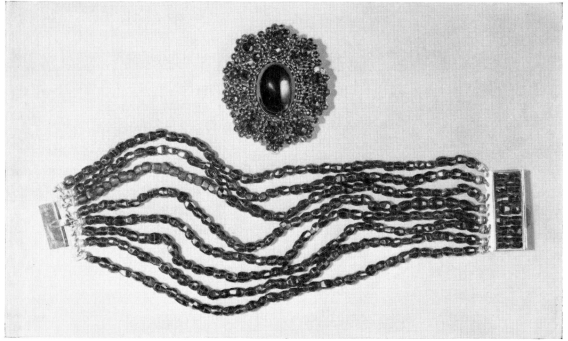

revival during the 1920s. As early as 1868, however, George Augustus Sala could make the following comment:

'Coral is a thing about which a great deal may be said, both for and against. Carelessly selected, clumsily set, and ignorantly arranged it may become one of the most vulgar and unsightly of known ornaments. Coral was in fact thus vulgarized a few years since in France and England. People went about bedizened with twisted sticks of seeming red sealing-wax; and coral ear-rings bore an unpleasant resemblance to fragments of ginger or orris-root, or even the domestic forked radish, smeared with red ochre.'

A great deal has been written about jet in recent years, and it remains one of the best-known materials used in Victorian popular jewellery. It was not only the Queen's lengthy mourning for Prince Albert which led to the rise of the Whitby jet industry, although her long widowhood did undoubtedly exert a social pressure that led to a widespread demand for mourning jewellery of all kinds. Jet jewellery was being produced in considerable quantity during the 1850s and the Whitby industry was well represented at the Great Exhibition. A typical display was that of Isaac Greenbury, Whitby: 'Jet necklaces with appendage attached. Bracelets. Brooches. Candlesticks. Pin-cushion. Ear-rings.'

A considerable amount of this Victorian jet jewellery still survives and, although most of it is too heavy and too funereal for modern taste, some pendant jet ear-rings and small jet cameos are not without attraction. The material not only takes on a fine high polish, but can also be cut and faceted like a precious stone. Some of the better-quality necklaces display faceted jet beads. The material sometimes called 'French Jet' is no more than black glass and can readily be detected. It has a hard bright glitter, quite unlike jet's velvety colour, and the glass imitation is cold to the touch. It is not vandalism to suggest that one of the best uses of a Victorian jet necklace is to restring it and intersperse the jet beads with modern paste roundels.

Hair jewellery was one of the strange and sentimental aberrations of the Early Victorian period. Little of it is left intact, despite the fact that at one time there were a number of London manufacturers engaged in the production of little else. This hair jewellery must be considered one of the more curious by-products of the Romantic Revolution and can hardly be considered even in terms of popular jewellery. As late as the mid-1850s William Cleal, of 53, Poland Street, was advertising as 'Manufacturer and Specialist in human hair jewellery'.

The Victorian period is above all notable for this rise of popular or mass-produced jewellery, most of which was designed for the lower and middle classes. The upper classes and the well-to-do, in their comfortable untaxed world, were still able to adorn their womenfolk with precious stones and metals. That a considerable amount of Victorian popular jewellery has survived into our own day can be put down to the fact that, even where they mass-produced, the Victorians insisted on weight and solidity.

The costume jewellery trinkets of the 20th century find their way into the rubbish-bin when their plating wears thin and their paste stones fall out. Victorian pieces, however, were designed to last, and many of them are worthy of the collector's attention.

6

Techniques and Materials

GOLD was the dominant precious metal of the Victorian era. Silver, which had been popular during the previous century for the setting of diamonds and precious stones, as well as pastes and marcasites, declined somewhat in favour. Platinum, although its properties were known, did not figure greatly in the sphere of the jeweller until the end of the century because of its great scarceness. (It was not, in fact, until the discovery of the great nickel-copper ore deposits in Ontario after the First World War that platinum became widely available.). Gold, however, was the Victorian metal *par excellence*. Its opulent associations and rich colour made it psychologically 'right' for the time. Improved technical methods made a wider range of coloured golds accessible to the working jeweller, and the use of delicately varied coloured golds is one of the hallmarks of the Victorian jeweller.

The quality of gold is determined in 'carats'—a form of measurement that assumes a completely pure gold as 24 carats. This pure gold, however, is too soft for the jeweller and the metal is alloyed to give it the necessary working hardness. For use with precious stones the standard gold used by the jeweller is 18 carats, although some Victorian jewellery will be found as pure as 22 carats, which is considered a little too soft today for satisfactory use. In cheaper articles, such as cameo mounts and brooch frames, 9-carat gold will be found—although less commonly than would be the case today, for the Victorians were not worried by the same economic restrictions which harass their descendants.

Red, white, green, pink, and blue golds are all found among

Victorian pieces. Red gold, one of the oldest coloured varieties used by the jeweller, is formed by the addition of a small percentage of copper to the refined ore; white gold by adding silver; blue by a percentage of iron; and green by the addition of silver or cadmium. The advantage of white gold was that, prior to the general use of platinum or palladium for diamond setting, white gold had nearly as high a degree of reflectivity as silver, with the added advantage that it did not tarnish. In the Late Victorian and Early Edwardian period white gold was increasingly used for important diamond-set pieces such as *rivières* and tiaras.

Second to gold among the world's precious metals—in terms of antiquity—is silver. Although silver had been widely used as a setting for precious stones during the 18th century, its use declined during the Victorian period as, firstly, white gold became more generally known and, secondly, platinum. The fact that silver tarnished easily militated against it during the Victorian period. This had not been a great drawback during earlier centuries when the atmosphere, even of London, was comparatively pure. But in the smoke of the new industrial cities women now found that silver settings needed to be cleaned constantly, as the sulphur in the atmosphere quickly tarnished the metal. It was this 'change of climate' which, almost as much as anything else, reduced the status of silver during the 19th century, so that, towards the end, it occupied something like the position that it does today—a setting primarily for second-grade jewellery.

Platinum was not widely used until the Edwardian era and after, but it is sometimes found as a setting for diamonds and precious stones during the last decades of the 19th century. Somewhat similar to silver in colour, but untarnishable, platinum takes its name from the Spanish *Platina del Pinto*, 'Little silver of the Pinto', the river in South America where it was first discovered. The technical problems involving the use of platinum prohibited its use until the 19th century and its great rarity kept it comparatively unknown until the 1890s. It was not until the technical advances of the Industrial Revolution that the extremely high melting-point of platinum (1,773° C.) could be mastered. Nowadays platinum, and its sister metal palladium, are the jeweller's first choice for diamond-setting. They are both highly reflective and possess the same untarnishable characteristic as gold.

Apart from the use of coloured golds, the Victorians were also fond of enamelling the metal. The influences of the revived Gothic and Renaissance styles were largely responsible for this demand for enamel-work. Painted enamel of 'Limoges' style was principally used by the Victorian jeweller. In this method the enamel is fused on to the prepared metal surface without the addition of any of the metal *cloisons* (or cells) which in earlier times had been considered essential to enamel-work. The basis of painted enamel is the use of vitreous glazes which have different melting-points; so that the one can be 'fired' after the other without causing the first to melt. Technical improvements such as this were part of the scientific revolution from which the Victorian jeweller benefited.

Enamel is a fused glass or other vitreous substance which is coloured with various metallic oxides, opaque enamels being achieved by the addition of tin to the mixture. The great architect and progenitor of the Gothic Revival, Augustus Welby Pugin (1812-1852), was largely responsible for this revival of interest in enamelling. The three mediaeval techniques in which Pugin interested himself were *cloisonné, champlevé*, and encrusted enamel. As a few examples of work in this manner may be found among extant Victorian jewellery, it is important for the collector and student to have a basic knowledge of the methods involved. The following is a clear exposition of the three techniques, and is of interest in that it is taken from a survey, *Birmingham and the Midland Hardware District*, compiled by W. C. Aitken in 1866.

'The enamels with which the old metal-worker had to do, and the use of which Pugin successfully laboured to revive, were the *cloisonné*, the *champlevé*, and the encrusted. The *cloisonné* is produced by fastening together with hard solder slender strips of metal which formed the outline of the subject to be represented. This metallic outline is soldered on a plate of metal, frequently gold; and before filling with enamel much resembles a pastry-cook's shape, for cutting leaves, etc. The spaces, or cells, are then filled in with enamel of various colours. The *champlevé*, on the contrary, was produced by cutting the design into the surface of the metal, the spaces to be filled with enamel being sunk, and the portions intended for the outline, or to separate the colours of the enamel, being left standing. The enamel itself is reduced to a granulated powder, and in this state is applied with a small spatula. When the incisions or troughs are filled with the various colours, the work is placed in a muffle, which is heated sufficiently to fuse the enamel into the spaces, the use of a muffle being necessary in order to prevent any injurious gases evolved by the fuel coming in contact with the enamel and spoiling its purity and brilliance. If, after fusing, the surface of the enamel is too far below the walls of the cell prepared for its reception, more is applied and fused. The whole is then ground down to the level of the surface of the metal, polished with hones, and finally "lapped" to secure brilliancy of finish.

'Encrusted enamel is applied to the surface of the metal without engraving, the various objects represented, leaves, fruit, flowers, figures, etc., being rendered in their natural colours. In this variety, the enamels are left with the "fire-glaze" produced by fusing still upon them without any after polishing.'

Somewhat akin to enamel and occasionally found in Victorian work is *niello*. *Niello*-work was much used in Renaissance jewellery and was revived during the 19th century, although never to any great extent. The metal surface of the required article, either of gold or silver (usually the latter), is engraved with the required design. The *niello*, which is a black metallic substance produced by the fusion of silver, lead, copper, and sulphur, is applied to the engraved surface and fused into the sunk lines by heating in the type of oven called a muffle. After this process is completed the piece is ground down and polished so that the article is left with an engraved design filled in with the black *niello*. Lockets and pendants were sometimes treated in this way during Victorian times, the design very often being copied from antique works or being pastiche copies of Renaissance designs. Somewhat similar to *niello* is damascening, where the lines left by the graving tool are filled in by threads of silver or gold wire. Originally employed for the decoration of arms and armour, damascening was sometimes used during the 19th century to decorate caskets and boxes.

Two terms which will often be encountered in descriptions of Victorian jewellery are 'filigree-work' and 'saw-piercing'. The former is the use of fine precious metal wire twisted and laid together so as to form geometric or naturalistic designs. It was very popular with the Victorian jeweller, the surrounds to whose gemstone settings were often composed of gold filigree-work. The effect, when the filigree had been done by a fine craftsman, is very delicate when set with stones such as amethyst or topaz.

'Saw-piercing' is the formation of certain sections of ornament by leaving apertures in thin plates of the metal, so as to produce a reticulated appearance. The craftsman sketches his design on the metal—a design that may be almost as airy as lace—drills holes wherever necessary, and then passes his jeweller's saw through the holes and cuts away the redundant metal. During the 19th century cheaper types of jewellery represented saw-piercing by the use of a punch and bed. 'A purely mechanical process,' as W. C. Aitken rightly comments, 'which can no more reproduce the infinite variety obtained by saw-piercing than cast iron can imitate the effect of wrought.'

Another technical term that will be found in silver- or gold-work is 'bossing' or *repoussé*. Although less common in jewellery than in silversmithing, *repoussé*-work is sometimes found in brooches, where a sufficient area of gold or silver enables the technique to be applied. It consists in 'working up' an area of metal so that it stands above the surface and displays its design in relief. Texture is given to the metal by matting tools, and the finer details are finished off with the graver. Naturalistic motifs, such as leaves surrounding a brooch, will quite often be found worked in this way. It should on no account be confused with die-stamping, which is a mechanized method of achieving something like the same effect, but with nothing like the same clarity, definition, or finish. Die-stamping became prevalent during the Victorian period for all types of cheaper work, especially mass-produced jewellery.

The electro-gilding of metals was another 19th-century innovation, but for all fine work craftsmen still used the old-fashioned amalgam process in which a paste, composed of gold in combination with mercury, is applied to the surface that is to be gilt. By the application of heat the mercury is made to evaporate and leave behind the gold deposit adhering to the metal.

Burnishing, the process whereby a metal is brought up to its full perfection of colour and finish, was still carried out by burnishers made of hard stones such as agate. Although mechanical polishing was common in Victorian times, the burnishing and polishing of fine-quality pieces were still carried out—as they are even today—by hand.

The process known as 'granulation', whereby patterns are composed exclusively of metal grains soldered on to the surface of an article, was extensively revived during the 19th century. This, as we have seen, was largely owing to the experimentation and researches of Fortunato Castellani into the methods employed by the ancient Etruscans.

In the tomb of Tutankhamen, ornaments made as early as 1350 B.C. with exquisitely fine granulation have been found—some of the applied gold grains being no more than one-sixteenth of an inch

(*Extreme left*) The tortoise, a motif popular in the 1880s. In gold set with a carbuncle. (*Left*) Gold brooch set with pearls, blue enamelling contrasted against 'bloomed' surfaces.

(*Right*) Gold brooch with 'blooming' and repoussé work. Note gipsy setting of diamond in centre.
(*Below*) Left, amethyst, diamond, and pearl ring. Right, amethyst and filigree gold brooch.

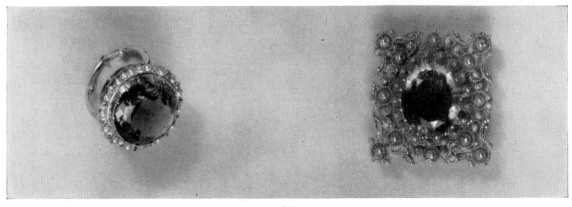

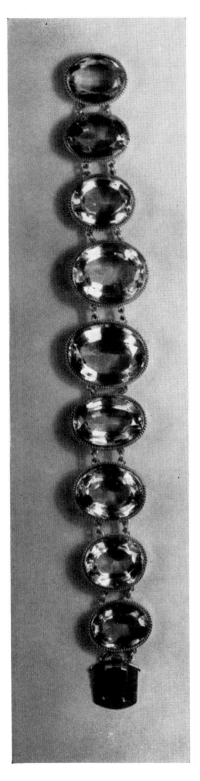

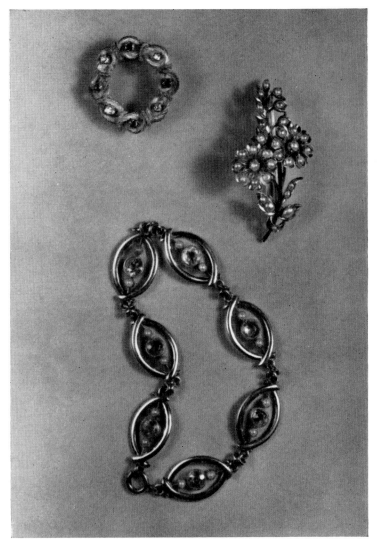

Top to bottom. Rope-work gold brooch set with diamonds and rubies; floral gold brooch with pearls; gold link bracelet with pearls and amethysts.

Simple link bracelet set with finely matched topaz.

in diameter. The Etruscans and the Greeks, however, improved on the Egyptians goldsmiths and often used grains as fine as one-hundredth of an inch. In some of the Etruscan work these minute gold grains are sprinkled so delicately on the surface that they look more like a 'bloom' on the metal than what they actually are—individual beads of gold.

H. Maryon and H. J. Plenderleith, in *A History of Technology* (Vol. I), describe the granulation on an Etruscan bowl, in which: 'There are more than 860 linear inches in the pattern, and over 137,000 grains are used. . . . The arrangement of the grains and the soldering of such small masses, without flooding or clogging them with solder, required very skilful manipulation'—such skilful manipulation, in fact, that the Etruscan work in granulation has never been bettered. The techniques used by the Castellanis have never been revealed, but modern researches have uncovered at least one method of achieving granulation as fine as Etruscan work. Unfortunately, the amount of man-hours involved and the excessive delicacy required make it unlikely that the 20th century will see a revival of this type of work. Today, as in the 18th century, the faceted stone is dominant in jewellery, and the craft of the goldsmith has been allowed to decay.

Maryon and Plenderleith have the following interesting points to make about the lost art of granulation: 'Many efforts to recover it were made during the late nineteenth century, but this work did not possess the delicacy and freedom of the old. The solder, however finely cut or filed, tended to flood the grains or wires, and the flux employed in the soldering was liable to boil up and displace the grains. The first difficulty was overcome by dividing the solder into even more minute particles—chemically rather than mechanically —and the second by omitting the flux altogether. A copper compound . . . was used with glue to fasten the grains or wires in place. When heated, the glue carbonized and the copper compound turned into copper oxide. The carbon then reduced the copper oxide to copper and disappeared as carbon monoxide, and a film of very finely divided copper was left in the joint. This alloyed with some of the adjacent gold, formed a solid, and joined the parts together. As a result of this discovery the investigator was able to copy some of the finest Etruscan and Greek jewels. . . .'

So much research has gone into the technique of granulation since the mid-19th century that we can still do no more than salute those ancient Etruscan craftsmen whose skill and artistry still mocks modern science. It is probable that, without knowing the chemical why and wherefore, something akin to the method outlined above was used by these early workmen. (On a recent visit to the island of Elba, I inspected the work of a local jeweller who was making granulated work akin to that of Castellani. He informed me that he used a type of simple fish glue to hold the beads in place during the heat process. The result was not quite as fine as Etruscan work, but very similar to the 19th-century Italian granulation.)

Although certain aspects of craftsmanship, such as granulation, engaged the jeweller's attention during this century and prompted him to concentrate on the finest details of his profession, it must not be forgotten that many of the commoner articles were deeply affected by the industrialization of the period. The finest pieces of gem-set jewellery remained works of art, but many of the lesser degrees came under the sway of the all-powerful machine. A survey of the jewellery trade carried out by J. S. Wright in the seventies gives one a clear picture of the effect of the machine upon the lesser ends of the trade:

'The application of dies and machinery . . . has contributed to the extraordinary extension of the trade. Formerly, the whole article was produced by one man, and was, consequently, very expensive; but, owing to the subdivision of labour, and the use of machines, articles formerly made in units are now produced in hundreds.

'Let us take a common ear-ring, or locket, for example. Under the old system the gold would have been beaten out by hand to the thickness required, and then forced into the proper shape by repeated hammering; the edges of the back and front filed that they might join correctly, after which it would be soldered and finished —all this being the work of one person.

'Now, a die is cut or engraved, the gold rolled at the steam mill to the requisite gauge, then blanks or discs are cut out by a screw-press, stamped and cut to the exact shape desired (also by the press) all this being done so rapidly that twenty are produced in the same time as one was formerly made.'

Another development during the century was the specialized mass-production of such *minutiae* as claw-settings and jewellers' 'findings' in general. Instead of having to make each and every setting individually, jewellers by the end of the century ordered their 'findings' from central suppliers. This was the beginning of the modern uniformity of setting, and the loss of a certain individuality even in expensive, precious pieces.

The following is a brief guide to the types of setting which will be found in Victorian pieces. First of all comes the *claw* setting, with which everyone will be familiar. Its name is self-explanatory, and it is principally used for the display of important stones.

The *millegrain* was very popular during the century, and is an attractive means of enhancing the apparent area of a sparkling stone such as the diamond. Innumerable tiny adjacent beads of metal are raised up to grip the girdle of the stone. It is somewhat similar to the *carved* setting fashionable during the 18th century, except that in the *millegrain* the back of the stone is left open, thus increasing the reflectivity. In the *carved* setting the stone was bedded in solid metal. The *carved* setting was used by the Victorians for opaque or dark-coloured stones, and was a common setting for brooch stones.

Pavé setting, also used in Victorian times and particularly for diamonds, is somewhat similar to *millegrain* except that the stones are set so close together that the metal dividing one stone from another can scarcely be distinguished. *Pavé* setting is seen at its best in the expanse of a large diamond brooch, where the whole area becomes a reflective mass of 'fire'.

The closed or *box* setting (the oldest in jewellery) was still used for *cabochon* stones. In this method the stone is held in a small box of metal, the edges of which are rubbed over to grasp the stone above the girdle. The old-fashioned *open* setting had more or less been superseded in Victorian times. It consisted of a *box*, the back of which had been cut away to permit the play of light through the stone.

Such are the basic settings to be found in Victorian jewellery. They differ little from those in use today, except that—especially in Early Victorian jewellery—a claw setting will usually have been made up by the jeweller himself.

The brilliant and the rose cut for diamonds have already been described. It is worth remembering that towards the end of the century the old-fashioned rose cut became widely fashionable and a considerable amount of Late Victorian diamond jewellery was set with rose-cut stones. Other main types of gem cutting which are likely to be found in 19th-century jewellery are: the *baguette*, a rectangular cut for small diamonds; the *briolette*, a pear-shaped drop cut with triangular facets; and the *cabochon*, where the top of the stone is rounded without facets. The *emerald* cut, also known as the step or trap cut, is usually oblong or square, with the facets arranged in a series of steps so as to display the full colour of the stone rather than effect a play of light. The *marquise* cut, or *navette* cut, is a pointed oval. The mixed cut in which the crown has much the same form as the brilliant, but the base is step cut with the proportions similar to a brilliant-cut *pavilion*, was used to produce both colour and brilliance. The *pendeloque* is a pear-shaped brilliant cut.

There are, of course, innumerable variants of these basic types of cutting. Many of these variants were evolved during the Victorian

Gold and mollusc shell cameo suite, with foliage and scroll borders.

Carved gems were popular in the second half of the century. Amethysts mounted in delicate filigree gold settings. Note the fine workmanship on back of ear-ring (*left centre*).

Topaz in the heavy,
opulent setting of the
mid-Victorian period.

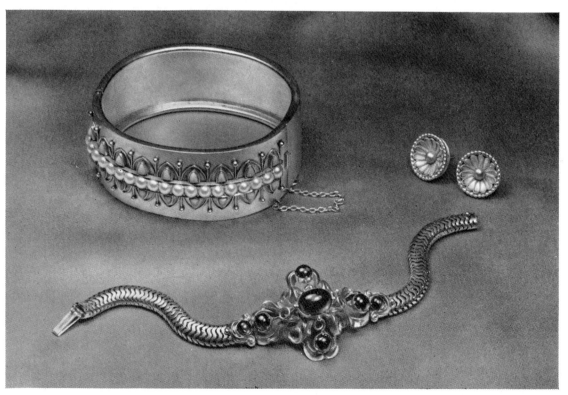

Gold bangle set with half pearls. Two gold stud ear-rings. Flexible gold bracelet
set with carbuncles.

period when the increased technical skill of the lapidary made him adventurous and experimental. The *briolette*, for instance, was a drop-shaped rose cut often favoured for gemstones used in pendant ear-rings.

It was during the 19th century that such technical improvements as the mechanically operated wheel and scientific research into the composition and cutting of gemstones elevated the faceted gemstone into the foremost place in jewellery. As the century advanced, despite the mediaeval and Renaissance yearnings of the Arts and Crafts Movement towards a greater emphasis on the mount and enamelled gold-work, the faceted gemstone came more and more to dominate the concept of precious jewellery. This trend, which was initiated as early as the 18th century, has gone so far that in our own day such important branches of the jeweller's craft as that of the enameller and the gold-worker have been almost entirely lost. More and more, as the Victorian period developed, the perfection of the jeweller's art was held to consist of fine gemstones, finely faceted and set in practically invisible mounts.

o o o o o
o 7 o
o o
o o o o o

The End of an Epoch

THE last years of the Victorian era were marked by two divergent trends in jewellery. The principal one, which was followed by most of the manufacturing jewellers, was distinguished by its use of platinum for diamond setting. The other, initiated by the students, craftsmen, and followers of the Arts and Crafts Exhibition Society, was a movement towards a Renaissance or mediaeval use of gold and silver, and a revival of enamelling.

Despite the fact that the Arts and Crafts Society attracted some considerable attention at the time, and that subsequent writers on the period have continued to take the movement at its own valuation, it is doubtful whether it had much effect on the ordinary working jeweller. It is also disputable whether the products of these amateurs were in any way finer, or artistically more satisfying, than the pieces made by the professionals.

In precious jewellery, the fashion at the end of the century was for very delicate 'invisible' settings with the maximum display of precious stones. The diamond, more than ever before, came to dominate the scene. A Late Victorian or Edwardian dinner party was a blaze of tiaras, hair ornaments, corsage sprays, and bracelets, all designed to give the diamond its maximum display.

The following notice from *The Queen* (December 2nd, 1899) gives a representative picture of the fashion and styles in precious jewellery: 'The tracery of the frost and the cobweb texture of lace would seem to have been the sources whence Messrs J. W. Benson's designers have drawn their inspiration for much of the diamond work which is now to be seen at 25, Old Bond Street. So delicate is the setting that it is almost imperceptible, and a wonderful effect of transparency is gained, while each line and curve is defined as it were in the scintillating gems alone. Some exquisite new hair ornaments are at this moment to be seen at Messrs Benson's, which in their glittering beauty recall nothing so much as the crystal shafts left by the fingers of the frost on grass and foliage. Here and there a pendant stone enhances the lustrous effect by increasing the varying play of light. The magnificent corsage ornament sketched brings to mind the beauty of a spray of flowers spangled with dewdrops. It may be worn entire or detached to form several brooches. A different style is shown in the scroll tiara of classic outline, softened by pendant collet stones. . . . A method revived with singular success by Messrs Benson is to set the brilliants in a "milled" edging of silver, which imparts a fine crinkled outline of extreme softness.'

Such jewellery was typical of the period. It is interesting to note that the suite of composite jewellery with its detachable brooches, bows, and small pendants was already fashionable. Composite jewellery of this type has become increasingly popular in our own century, though mainly for reasons of economy such as scarcely bothered our Victorian ancestors. Elsewhere in the same issue of this magazine the correspondent describes what is termed 'Artistic Jewellery'. The word 'artistic' is prevalent in descriptions of the crafts during this period, and is one of the concessions which the manufacturers made to the Arts and Crafts Movement. 'Art silks', 'Art furnishings', and 'Art jewellery' are terms that abound in the advertisements of the time. The following is a description of some of the pieces termed 'Artistic Jewellery': '. . . the new Creole earrings in plain gold; others set with pearls or *cabochon* rubies, as well as those formed entirely of *à jour* set [open at the back so that the light shines through] brilliants. Chain bangles of Oriental character set with uncut rubies, emeralds, and other gems, several different stones appearing in one bangle, are both unique and artistic.'

Whereas the work of the manufacturing jewellers tended to become more and more light and fragile, the followers of the Arts and Crafts Movement concentrated on 'chunky' settings, *cabochon* stones, and enamel-work. They were fond of silver for their settings —either carved, engraved, or *repoussé*.

It is not surprising that there should be something of an amateurish feeling about so much of this work. What is surprising is that, whenever the arts and crafts of the Victorian period are displayed on exhibition (as in the Victoria and Albert Museum in 1952), it is only the products of these somewhat self-conscious artists and craftsmen which are shown. In itself, this is a convincing argument for the success of the Arts and Crafts Exhibition Society if, whenever the handcrafts of the period are under consideration, it is the products of the Society which automatically come to mind. The fact remains that this occurs principally because the Society was an extremely vocal and well-publicized group.

To attempt to place the products of the Arts and Crafts Movement in correct perspective with the general pattern of the age is not to denigrate their achievement. It is time, however, that they were seen as what indeed they were—a self-conscious and self-aware group of artists and amateurs whose achievements, though not without ·merit, had very little effect on the jewellery and metalwork of the period.

William Morris himself was fully conscious of the unavoidable limitations of the Society. The crux of their problem cannot be better expressed than when Morris put in his preface to *Art and Crafts Essays* (1893): 'We can expect no general impulse towards the fine arts till civilization has been transformed into some other condition of life, the details of which we cannot foresee. Let us then make the best of it, and admit that those who practise art must nowadays be conscious of that practice; conscious I mean that they are either adding a certain amount of artistic beauty and interest to a piece of goods which would, if produced in the ordinary way, have no beauty or artistic interest, or that they are producing something

Three of the pieces of A. W. N. Pugin jewellery as made up by Hardman
of Birmingham for the 1851 Exhibition.

111

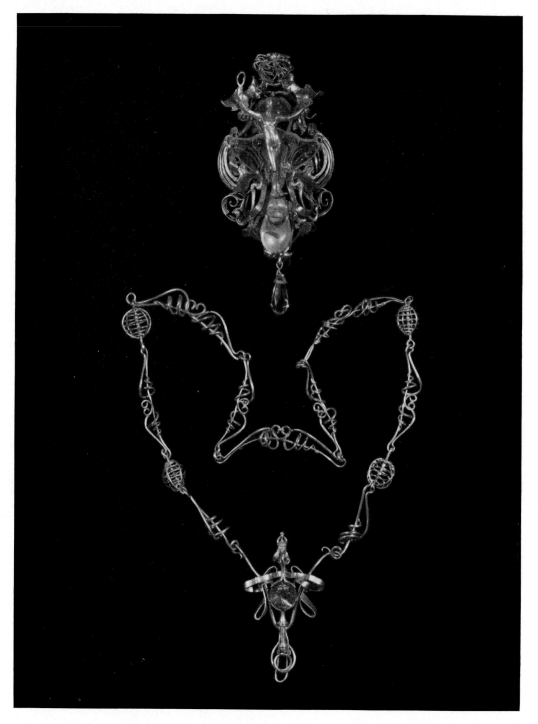

Presidential badge and chain by Alfred Gilbert, 1901. The influence of
Art Nouveau is to be seen in the linear convolutions of the design.

112

which has no other reason for existence than its beauty and artistic interest.'

That is well said, but what seems disputable is whether the jewellery of C. R. Ashbee, Henry Wilson, or Phoebe Traquair was of any greater artistic value than some of the standard pieces made by professional jewellers such as Brogden, Garrard, and Phillips. These Late Victorian and Early Edwardian clips and brooches were 'produced in the ordinary way', but some of them have almost as much elegance and charm as the much-prized pieces of the 18th century.

In one respect, at least, it must be regretted that the Arts and Crafts Society did not have more influence upon their age, and this was in their attempt to revive the craft of enamelling. Some of the work by Omar Ramsden, Harold Stabler, and Phoebe Traquair was technically excellent, even if their designs were less satisfactory. Unfortunately, the tide of fashion was against them. The glamour of the faceted stone set in 'invisible' settings carried everything before it. The ordinary customer was no longer interested in a decorative, colourful setting, but wanted impeccably-cut gemstones, displayed with the maximum amount of reflected light.

Holbrook Jackson in *The Eighteen-Nineties* (1913) aptly summed up the dilemma of the Arts and Crafts Movement: 'The outward effect of this search for excellence of quality and utility in art was, however, not so profound as it might have been. This is explained by the fact that the conditions under which Morris and his group worked were so far removed from the conditions of the average economic and industrial life of the time as to appear impractical for general adoption. They demonstrated, it is true, that it was possible to produce useful articles of fine quality and good taste even in an age of debased industry and scamped counterfeit workmanship; but their demonstration proved also that unless something like a revolution happened among wage-earners none but those of ample worldly means could hope to become possessed of the results of such craftsmanship.'

So many of the products of these followers of Morris were also to become unpleasantly tainted by the influence of *Art Nouveau*. Their spidery and attenuated figures, their twisting leaves, and 'Beardsley' scroll-work were certainly little, if at all, better than the somewhat mechanical classicism of the professional jewellers. In the sphere of precious jewellery, which had in any case been less contaminated by the Industrial Revolution than the other crafts, the price factor had ensured that a diamond necklace was still a masterpiece of craftsmanship, even if its design might be hackneyed.

The jewellery of the Arts and Crafts Society fell between two stools. It was neither glamorous enough, nor fashionable enough, for the rich and fashionable; and it was too expensive for the masses. The designer of mass-produced jewellery (always provided that his designs were good ones) came nearer to fulfilling Morris's dream of putting articles of quality and taste within the reach of ordinary people.

The Aesthetic movement, however, did exert a considerable influence on dress fabrics and colours, and this was reflected in the jeweller's palette. The trade journal, *The Watchmaker, Jeweller, and Silversmith*, has the following fashion note in 1886: 'The rage for aesthetic colours in dress fabrics is also producing a demand for soft-coloured stones such as peridot, tourmaline, Alexandrite, spinel, and fancy-coloured sapphires, which is causing these stones to fetch fair prices. Mounted with diamonds they are effective.'

Novelty was the cry at the end of the epoch—novelty in design, material, and conception. One finds hair ornaments with quivering stalks ('powered by a Voltaic battery concealed on the person') and a profusion of animal, bird, and insect motifs used in both precious and popular jewellery. 'The miniature bat,' we read in an issue of *The Queen* for 1899, 'with ruby body and diamond wings, swinging from a fine gold chain set with pearls, illustrates the latest fashion in lace pins, in which the same idea is carried out with a jewelled tortoise.' The Paris jewellers went a stage farther and bejewelled real tortoises—a conception which shocked a correspondent to the trade magazine. 'Who but a Parisian would conceive the idea of bejewelling a live tortoise?' he asked. 'The little animal must obey the dictates of nature and consequently the very idea of wearing a live thing on the person is repugnant.'

The innumerable insect brooches which are still to be found in second-hand shops largely date from the last decade of the 19th century. Every conceivable kind of beetle and butterfly, as well as lizards, bats, birds, exotic flowers, ferns, and fish, were used as motifs for jewelled clips set with semi-precious stones and small diamonds. Some of these clips and brooches are very delicate and finely worked, others are merely run-of-the-mill productions which were turned out in their hundreds.

Another freak fashion, which unfortunately destroyed many fine old 18th-century watches, was to dismantle the finely engraved parts of the watch and set them as necklaces and even ear-rings. The first reference to this fashion in England occurs in *The Watchmaker, Jeweller, and Silversmith* of September, 1886. The modern watch-collector may well grieve when he learns that the fashion quickly crossed the Channel. 'Passing down the Rue St Honoré yesterday, I noticed a very neat, tasteful and original show of jewellery made entirely out of the works of old watches. . . . The cock has been made up into ear-rings, brooches, necklaces, heads for hairpins, and gentleman's scarf-pins . . . and heavily plated for its new ornamental purposes.'

The Edwardian period saw the triumph of platinum as the ideal metal for the setting of precious stones. From 1900 onwards platinum was almost exclusively used as a setting for diamonds. It was the metal's greater hardness and brightness which enabled it so rapidly to supersede silver. In addition, the metal was light and enabled the fashionable delicate designs to be carried out in quite large expanses without 'dragging down' dress materials. The delicacy of the settings meant that jewellers tended to use larger stones than before, when silver with 'illusion' settings had been used. Sun-ray tiaras became fashionable, and the lightness of platinum meant that brooches could be made larger than in the past. The stomacher, a descendant of the *Sévigné*, but covering almost the whole front of the dress, was another offshoot of the platinum revolution. Inevitably, after two world wars and the breaking up of many family fortunes, the more important pieces of diamond jewellery from this era have nearly all been recast into new forms and modes.

It is interesting to note that the craftsman who almost seems to personify the Edwardian age was French by descent, even though he was Russian by birth. Peter Carl Fabergé has been exalted in recent years into something approaching a cult. Two biographies have been written about him, and the steady increase in sale-room prices of Fabergé articles is—as much as anything else—a witness to the modern nostalgia for that prosperous and secure age. Most of Fabergé's work cannot compare with the excellence of the 18th century, and a great deal of it is disfigured by an Edwardian vulgarity. On the other hand, he was the epitome of his age and probably the last of the great international jewellers. He has been compared to Cellini by his admirers, but the comparison will not stand analysis. Nevertheless, Carl Fabergé, in so far as he marks the climax and the end of a period, deserves his place in this record. He had his own establishment in London, and so much of his jewellery was bought by the fashionable—as well as copied by the London jewellers of the time—that his influence cannot be discounted.

He was born in St Petersburg in 1846, the son of a jeweller, and he died seventy-four years later in exile in Lausanne. In the long span of his life he witnessed the heyday of Victorian and Edwardian prosperity, as well as the extinction of the society that had made his craft possible. In the course of his life he saw the final flowering of the Age of Luxury, not only in Russia but throughout Europe. His had been the strange, secret knowledge of the jeweller—as intimate almost as the confessional. He had made jewelled Easter

Eggs for the Tsars, over fifty of them in the course of thirty-five years; gold cigarette-cases for King Edward VII, models in semi-precious stone of the Sandringham animals for Queen Alexandra; and jade Buddhas for the King of Siam. No craftsman was ever more lucky in his patrons. Even Benvenuto Cellini, at the height of the Renaissance, had a hard job to find clients, but Fabergé was courted and sought after as no jeweller ever was before—and most probably never will be again.

Although the Fabergé family had been in Russia for nearly 200 years, they were of Huguenot stock, and Carl Fabergé was himself sent to Paris for his education. It is a curious fact that the rise of the House of Fabergé was largely due to the patronage of the Tsar Alexander III, a ruthless and autocratic Emperor of whom Queen Victoria remarked that 'He is a sovereign whom we do not look upon as a gentleman.' Yet he possessed an instinct, which fortunately many despots have shared, of being a great patron of the arts. From the moment that he appointed the House of Fabergé court jewellers and goldsmiths, their fortune was made. The talent and the business acumen of Carl Fabergé soon saw to it that their products became a byword throughout Europe.

John Addington Symonds, writing of Cellini, made the wise remark that 'Artists who aspire to immortality must shun the precious metals'; and his words remain true for all who practise the craft of goldsmith or jeweller. Yet, despite the fact that a lot of Fabergé's work has inevitably been destroyed during the past forty years, there are still a number of pieces on the market both in England and the Continent. They range from *minuterie* like parasol handles and pencil-cases to large objects of fantasy such as the Imperial Easter Eggs.

If the Easter Eggs may be said to represent the most exotic productions of Fabergé, the fact remains that much of his finest work is to be found in smaller articles. The limitations of the medium—in pieces such as cigarette-cases and trinkets—restrain a Russian

117

tendency towards Byzantine extravagance. Fabergé's cases, powder-boxes, fan-holders, and other kinds of smallwork reveal a grace and elegance which can almost equal similar productions of the French 18th-century craftsmen. If it is not too fanciful to trace a personal ancestry through the workshops of Fabergé (which employed over 700 men), then it would seen that in these items of small work there is a trace of that Gallic good taste which he inherited from his ancestors and from his early training.

The prosperity of that Late Victorian and Edwardian world was such that Fabergé was able to maintain workshops in Moscow, St Petersburg, Odessa, and Kieff, as well as a branch of the business in London. Inevitably, as the head of so large and prosperous a firm, Fabergé became somewhat divorced from the work-bench. Although it was still his custom to 'pass' practically every piece that went out into the world bearing his hall-mark, he employed other designers to work for him. The only English craftsman who appears ever to have been employed by Fabergé was Alfred Pocock, a modeller and carver, who is still alive and still at work in this country. Pocock was first engaged as a student to model some of the animals at Sandringham for the collection of Queen Alexandra. The models were then sent to St Petersburg to be carved in semi-precious stones by Fabergé's craftsmen.

Apart from the Easter Eggs, the jewellery, and the small work in general, one of the most attractive and unusual products of the House of Fabergé were artificial flowers, carved in precious and semi-precious stones. There was a vogue for such artificial flowers in the Edwardian period, and a number of London and Parisian jewellers made similar pieces—though rarely of anything approaching the same quality. A typical example of a Fabergé piece has a spray of flowers resting in a rock-crystal vase, the flowers themselves being made in rhodonite and white chalcedony, the leaves in nephrite, and the stalk in gold. A basket of lilies of the valley has leaves of nephrite, flowers in pearls and rose-cut diamonds, and the stalks, the moss, and the basket in different coloured golds.

Technically, the products of Fabergé are often superb. In terms of taste, they cannot be said to equal the work of the best English and French jewellers of the 19th century. Where Froment-Meurice, Giuliano, Phillips, and others have a certain restraint or classicism even in their more elaborate work, Fabergé with his Russian background was prone to a somewhat Oriental extravagance.

It is doubtful whether the world will ever know another jeweller of his stature. Like the last Tsar of All the Russias, he belongs to history. It is not difficult to see the injustice behind the world that gave birth to Fabergé, but some of his work will endure—like the pyramids in miniature—for as long as men care for the crafts of luxury and elegance. Nothing like it will ever be seen again, for the society which made it possible is ended. His last recorded words were: 'This is life no more.'

Fabergé and his work have been considered at some length for he seems to epitomize both the achievements and the failures of the Late Victorian and Edwardian period. There were other jewellers in London and Paris who were as fine craftsmen, and many who specialized in similar trinkets, enamelled *objets d'art*, and other *minuterie* of the age. None of them, however, was a jeweller on so vast a scale. It is extremely doubtful whether the world will ever again witness such an international *arbiter elegantiarum*. On that day in the First World War when the Fabergé workshops were turned over to the manufacture of small-arms and shells, a whole epoch came to an end.

Conclusion

THERE is a growing tendency today to romanticize the Victorian era. Many eyes are turned back towards its security, its prosperity, and its tranquillity with an ever-deepening nostalgia. We have come a long way from the critics and the biographers of the 1920s who could find little good to say about the period, and whose reputations were made out of a denigration of its characters and achievements. We are in danger of following the swing of the pendulum too far in the opposite direction, if we do no more than reverse the process. The Victorian arts and crafts were subjected to a stress and strain that were unique in the history of mankind. Only today, and only slightly and in certain spheres, are we learning to overcome some of the difficulties with which the Victorians were confronted—and which were unique in that they had no examples from the past to guide them.

The Victorians were confronted with the Machine Age and with the complete change of human living that it brought in its train. They were confronted also with a change in social values, the rise of a prosperous middle class, and the growth of a new class altogether—the industrial worker. Significantly, it was the craft which could least suffer from industrialization that declined least aesthetically during the period. Jewellery, precious jewellery that is to say, was something which could not be manufactured by machines. Its initial cost, in terms of materials, was such that the additional cost of man-hours of specialized labour could not affect it. That is why—more than any other of the crafts—the products of the Victorian jeweller suffered so little under the first onslaught of the Industrial Revolution.

It may be only a nostalgic fancy that can prompt people to admire Berlin wool-work or Victorian Gothic wood-carving, but it is more than that which must compel our admiration for some of

120

A well-made necklace and brooch designed by Arthur Gaskin, 1908. Followers of the Arts and Crafts Movement always tended to ignore the fact that pieces like these, however well made and attractive in their own right, were unsuited to the fashions of the day.

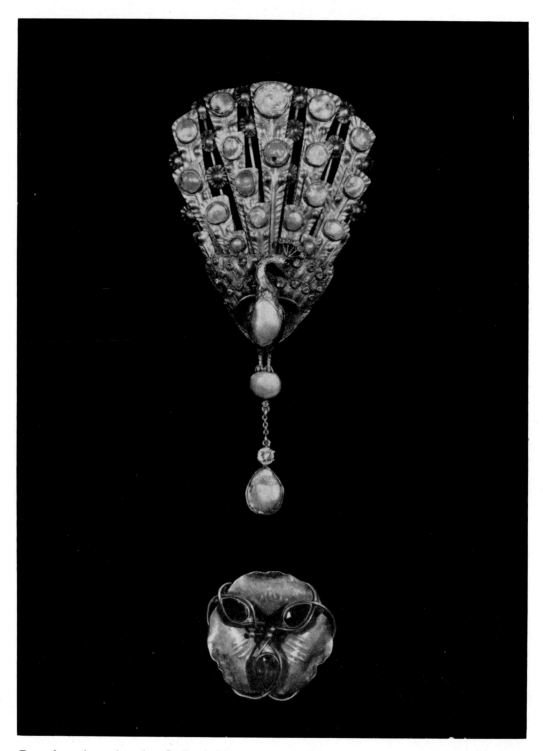

Brooch and pendant by C. R. Ashbee, *c.* 1900. The influence of *Art Nouveau* can be seen in the design while, in imitation of Renaissance work, the peacock's body is formed by a baroque pearl.

the products of the Victorian jeweller. In his intelligent use of coloured stones, of coloured golds, and of gold granulated and gold filigree work, the jeweller of the 19th century made a permanent contribution to the craft. He was, undoubtedly, aided by technical advances resulting from the Industrial Revolution. Improvements in lapidary work and in scientific gemmology were contributory to his success. He was fortunate that he was not swamped by the machine, but jewellery of quality—then as now—remains a craft which can be exercised only by a trained combination of human hand and eye.

In the sphere of jewellery, the most significant feature of the age was the growth of popular jewellery—the forerunner of the 'costume' or 'fashion' jewellery of our own age. Much of this has of course disappeared, but what remains should remind us of the fact that the Victorian jewellery craftsman had his roots deep in an old tradition. Even when he was forced to 'skimp' and work cheap, he worked to a higher standard and with a view to a more lasting product than is common today.

Many pieces of Victorian jewellery are deplorable in design, many are too heavy for today's dress fashions, but few of them are lacking in the great essential—craftsmanship. We live in an age when the immediate appearance, or performance, is all that counts. Our standards are the tawdry standards of the mass-production belt—and we would do well to realize that more hand-craftsmanship and more real care went into a Victorian ring than into a modern motor-car.

To end, as we began, with a quotation from Robert Browning, —the collector, the student, and the woman of taste can still find in many a second-hand shop in this country:

The rondure brave, the lilied loveliness,
Gold as it was, is, shall be evermore:
Prime nature with an added artistry—
No carat lost, and you have gained a ring.

Glossary

AIGRETTE: A hair ornament, in the form of a spray or plume, usually of gold or silver set with pearls or gemstones.

ALBERT: A gold chain for a man's watch, called after the Prince Consort.

ANNEALING: Toughening and softening metal by heating to make it malleable.

ARABESQUES: Flowing lines, leaves, and scroll-work, often in low relief.

ASSAY: The testing of metals to ensure that they are of a standard fineness.

ASTERISM: The six- or twelve-pointed star effect seen in certain gemstones—usually ruby or sapphire—and visible when they are cut *en cabochon* in the correct direction. Star-stones are also known as 'asterias'.

BAGUETTE: A rectangular cut for small diamonds, similar in shape to batons but smaller.

BALAS RUBY: A misnomer for red spinel.

BANGLE: A bracelet of solid gold, silver, or base metal, but not flexible.

BAROQUE PEARLS: Irregularly shaped pearls (Portuguese *barroco*: a rough pearl.)

BASSE-TAILLE: Also known as translucent enamelling. The design is cut in relief in the metal, and the cavities filled with translucent enamel so that an effect of light and shade is achieved, palest where the high parts of the design are only just covered, deepest at the bases of the cavities.

BEZEL: The groove or flange holding a gemstone in its setting or a watch-glass in place. Also the first four oblique facets of a gemstone cut after the table facet.

BIJOUTERIE: The craft of the goldsmith and enameller, as opposed to *joaillerie*, the craft of the mounter and gem-setter.

BLISTER PEARL: Irregularly shaped swellings of nacre, often hollow, within the shell of the pearl-bearing oyster.

BORT: Small fragments of diamond, too small for use in jewellery, which are crushed and used as abrasives.

BOX SETTING: A closed form of setting in which the gemstone is enclosed in a 'box' and the edges of the metal pressed down to hold the stone in place.

BRILLIANT CUT: The best type of cut for the diamond, used also for coloured stones such as zircon. The modern brilliant has a larger table or top facet than the Victorian cut, and has thirty-three facets above the girdle, twenty-five in the base.

BRIOLETTE: A pear-shaped drop cut for gemstones. The facets are all triangular.

BRISTOL STONE: Rock-crystal or colourless quartz. Sometimes erroneously applied to paste.

BRUTING: The method of roughly fashioning a diamond by rubbing two diamonds one against the other.

BULLION: Gold or silver before manufacture.

CABOCHON: The oldest method of cutting gemstones still in use. The top of the stone is rounded, without facets. The base may be concave, convex, or flat. Used for opaque, imperfect, and star-stones.

CAMEO: A carved gem or shell in which the carved design stands out against a darker or lighter background. (*See* Intaglio).

CARAT: The standard weight used for gemstones, equivalent to one-fifth of a gramme; also the measure of fineness of a gold alloy, pure gold being assessed at twenty-four parts.

CHAMPLEVÉ: A style of enamelling in which the ground is cut out to receive the enamel in powder form before firing. A strip of the metal is left between the scooped-out portions.

CHASING: The method of decorating silver or gold, using punches and a hammer. There are two distinct types of chasing—flat and *repoussé*. Flat or surface chasing is done from the front, giving definition to the metal but not cutting into it (which is engraving). *Repoussé* chasing is done by bulging out the metal from behind, then bringing out the detail by flat chasing from the front.

CHATELAINE: An ornamental chain, hung from the girdle or from a brooch, from which were suspended small objects such as scissors, keys, and seals.

CHATOYANCY: The cat's-eye effect seen in chrysoberyl cut *en cabochon* in the proper direction. Also seen in some quartzes.

CLAW-SET: A method of mounting gemstones in which minute 'claws', sometimes mounted on a 'coronet', hold down the crown facets.

CLEAVAGE: The property of certain gemstones, such as diamond and topaz, to split along one or more definite directions, parallel to a possible crystal face.

CLOISONNÉ: Cell-enamelling, in which narrow strips of gold or silver wire are bent to form cells and soldered to the base, the *cloisons* or compartments being filled with enamel.

COLLET SET: A development of box-setting in which the sides of the box are filed down to expose more of the gemstone to the light.

CREOLE EAR-RING: A metal ear-ring in the shape of a hoop or circle, the lower half of the circle usually being thicker than the upper.

CROWN: The upper part of a cut gemstone.

CULET: The small facet (sometimes omitted) at the base of a diamond. Not often found in stones cut in the 19th century.

DIAMANTÉ: White paste used for imitation jewellery.

DOUBLET: A composite stone consisting of two genuine stones, or one genuine and one imitation, cemented together so as to appear to be one large genuine stone.

EMERALD CUT: The step or trap cut, usually oblong or square, the

Queen Victoria. By Bertha Muller, after Heinrich von Angeli.

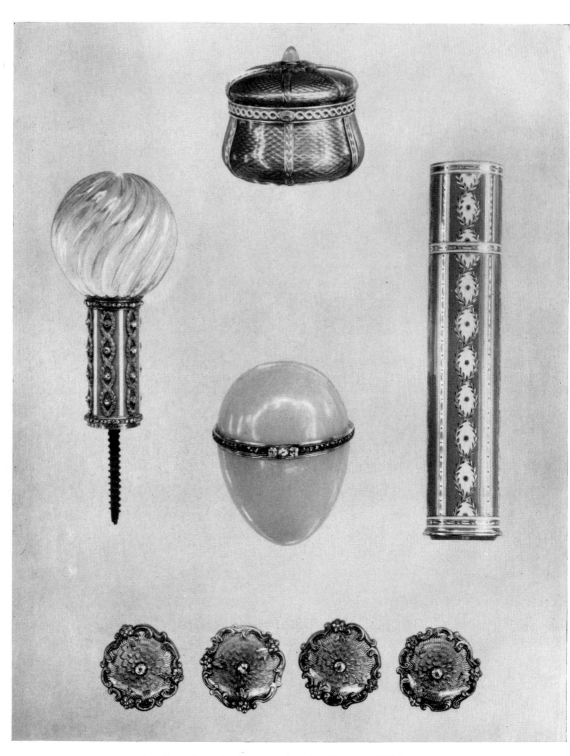

Smallwork and minuterie by the House of Fabergé.

facets being arranged in a series of steps to display the full colour of the stone rather than to effect brilliant play of light.

ENGRAVING: A linear pattern achieved by cutting away the surface of the metal with a sharp-pointed tool called a graver.

FACET: One of the small flat surfaces of a cut gemstone.

FEDE RING: Ring with a central motif of two clasped hands to symbolize troth. (Latin *fides*: trust, faith.)

FERRONIÈRE: A brow ornament. (From Leonardo da Vinci's *La Belle Ferronière.*)

FILIGREE: Delicate thread-like decoration in gold or silver wire.

FIRE: Flashes of colour emanating from the facets of a cut gemstone.

FLINT GLASS: Glass containing lead oxide, sometimes used for paste jewellery because of its brilliance, but rather soft and easily scratched.

FLUX: The fusible surface of an enamel; any substance mixed with metal to facilitate its fusion, as in soldering.

FOIL: A thin leaf of metal placed behind a gemstone or a paste in order to heighten its brilliance or strengthen its colour.

FRESHWATER PEARL: The product of the pearl-bearing mussel (*Unio margaritiferus*). Found in Great Britain in the rivers Tay and Spey.

GIPSY SETTING: A setting in which the top of the gemstone is scarcely above the level of the surrounding metal, which is sometimes engraved in a star pattern as though the rays emanated from the gemstone.

GIRANDOLE: A type of pendant ear-ring having three pear-shaped drops hanging from a large stone set at the top.

GIRDLE: The line dividing the crown or top of a faceted gemstone from the pavilion or base.

GLYPTIC: The art of carving and engraving gems.

GRAIN: In troy weight there are 480 grains to the ounce. A pearl grain, on the other hand, is a weight equivalent to one-quarter of a carat.

GRANULATED WORK: *Granaglia*. Work in which minute beads or granules of gold form a raised surface decoration.

GRAVER: The sharp tool used by the engraver to cut into the metal.

GRISAILLE: Painting in grey monochrome, sometimes used in enamel-work.

ILLUSION SETTING: Setting in which the edges of the metal surrounding the stone, usually a very small diamond, are cut or shaped so that they appear to be part of the gemstone itself, and apparently enhance its size.

INTAGLIO: A carved design hollowed out of the surface of the gem, as opposed to the cameo in which the background is cut away.

IN THE ROUND: In which the representation stands right away from the background, as distinct from in relief.

JEWELLERS' ROUGE: A powdered oxide of iron haematite, used for final polishing.

JOAILLERIE: *See* Bijouterie.

LAP: The lapidary's horizontal wheel, used for grinding and for polishing gemstones.

LUNATE: Crescent-shaped.

LUSTRE: The effect produced by the reflection of light from the surface of a gemstone. Most transparent stones have a vitreous lustre. Diamond is adamantine; marcasite metallic; amber resinous; etc.

MARCASITE: The name popularly given to iron pyrites when used for jewellery. True marcasite is rare and has a different crystal structure.

MARQUISE: A ring composed of a cluster of stones pointed at either end and covering the finger as far as the joint. Marquise cut, or navette cut, is a pointed oval.

MILLEGRAIN: A setting in which minute adjacent beads of metal grip the girdle of the stone.

MINUTERIE: Smallwork generally. Small pieces, such as rings and clips, produced by punching.

MIXED CUT: A cut with the crown having much the same form as the brilliant, the base being step cut but with similar proportions to a brilliant-cut pavilion.

MOHS'S SCALE: An order of hardness for gemstones devised by the mineralogist, Mohs.

NIELLO: A black compound of silver, copper, etc., used to fill in the engraved portions of silver and other metals.

PAILLONS: Small pellets of solder.

PARURE: A suite of matching jewellery.

PASTE: Glass usually containing a proportion of lead oxide and cut to resemble gemstones.

PAVÉ SETTING: A setting in which the stones are placed close together so that very little metal shows between them.

PAVILION: The lower section of a cut gemstone, below the girdle.

PENDELOQUE: A pear-shaped brilliant cut.

PINCHBECK: An alloy of copper and zinc used in imitation jewellery to simulate gold. Invented by watchmaker Christopher Pinchbeck, in the early 18th century.

PLIQUE-À-JOUR: A method of enamelling in which the backing is removed or cut away so that the light shines through in the manner of a stained-glass window.

REPOUSSÉ: Decoration on silver or gold achieved by pushing out the metal into relief from behind.

RHINESTONE: A modern misnomer for paste (particularly white paste) jewellery. Properly rock-crystal.

RIVIÈRE: A necklace made of a row of graduated single stones, usually diamonds.

ROSE CUT: A flat-based cut covered with triangular facets, usually twenty-four in number.

SEED-PEARL: A small round pearl weighing less than a quarter of a grain.

SÉVIGNÉ: A bodice ornament, often lavishly set with stones, in gold or silver. (After Mme de Sévigné, the French letter-writer.)

SHANK: The hoop of a ring.

SMALLWORK: Small objects of vertu, such as cigarette-cases, snuff-boxes, parasol handles, etc.

STRASS: A lead glass used for diamond imitations (After the 18th-century jeweller, Josef Strass.)

SUITE: A matching set of jewellery.

SYNTHETIC STONES: Manufactured stones having the same composition, crystal structure, and other properties as the natural mineral they represent.

TABLE: The top flat facet of a diamond or other gemstone, considerably larger in the 20th-century brilliant cut than in Victorian and earlier brilliants.

Selected Bibliography

Aitken, W. C. *Birmingham and the Midland Hardware District.* 1866.

Album of Arts and Industries of Great Britain. 1887.

Art Journal. 1849-1901.

Art Journal Catalogues of the International Exhibitions of 1851, 1855, 1862, and 1867.

Arts and Crafts Essays. 1893.

Bainbridge, H. C. *The Life and Work of Carl Fabergé.* 1950.

Blanc, C. *L'art dans la Parure et dans le Vêtement.* Paris, 1874.

Bradford, E. *Contemporary Jewellery and Silverware.* 1950.

Bradford, E. *Four Centuries of European Jewellery.* 1953.

Brown, W. N. *Art of Enamelling on Metal.* 1900.

Castellani, A. *Antique Jewellery and its Revival.* 1862.

Cunynghame, H. *The Art of Enamelling on Metals.* 1906.

Encyclopaedia of the Home. Cassell. 1900.

Flower, M. *Victorian Jewellery.* 1951.

Havard, H. *Histoire de l'Orfèvrerie Française.* Paris. 1896.

Haweis, H. R. *The Art of Beauty.* 1878.

Jackson, H. *William Morris.* 1908.

Jackson, H. *The Eighteen-Nineties.* 1913.

Labarte, J. *Histoire des Arts Industriels.* 1875.

Mayhew, H. *Life and Labour of the London Poor.* 1864.

Official Illustrated Catalogue of the Great Exhibition. 1851.

Pugin, A. W. N. *Glossary of Ecclesiastical Ornament.* 1844.

Prosser, W. *Birmingham Inventions.* 1881.

Reports of Artisans on the Paris Universal Exhibition. 1867.

Sala, G. A. *Notes and Sketches of the Paris Exhibition.* 1868.

Selwyn, A. *Retail Jewellers' Handbook.* 1951.

Snowman, K. *Carl Fabergé.* 1954.

Wallis, G. *British Manufacturing Industries*. 1877.
Watchmaker, Jeweller, and Silversmith, The. 1875-1900.
Webster, R. *Practical Gemmology*. 1941.
Wright, J. S. *The Jewellery and Gilt Toy Trades*. 1866.
Wyatt, Sir M. D. *Journal of Design*. 1851.

Index

Figures in bold type refer to pages in which illustrations appear.

Abercrombie, Lady, portrait of Queen
Victoria by, **45**

Aesthetic Movement, influence of
the, 51

Agate, brief account of, 60
drops in necklace and ear-rings, **55**

Aigrette, defined, 124
set with diamonds and turquoise, **18**

Aitken, W. C., 95

Albert, 124

*Album of the Arts and Industries of
Great Britain* (1887), 56

Alexandra, Queen, model animal
collection of, 118

Alexandrite, 58
brief account of, 60

Amber, 63

Amethyst, bracelet set with, **105**
brief account of, 63
brooches set with, **34, 67, 78, 99, 100**
cartouche set with, **62**
ear-rings set with, **77, 105**
necklaces set with, **61, 77, 84, 105**
popularity of, 29, 57, 58
rings set with, **61, 83, 99**

Angeli, Heinrich von, portrait of Queen
Victoria after, **45**

Animal motifs, **40**

Annealing, 124

Apprenticeship system, high standard
of, 19

Aquamarine, 63

Arabesques, 124

Art and Craft Essays (1895), 110

Arts and Crafts, Victorian, position of,
summed up by Sir Matthew Digby
Wyatt, 26

Arts and Crafts Exhibition Society, 108,
110, 113
jewellery of, 114

Ashbee, C. R., designer, 52, 113
brooch and pendant by, **122**

Assay, 124

Assyrian motifs, introduced into English
jewellery, 26

Asterism, 124

Backes and Strauss, manufacturers of
facsimiles of ancient works, 37

Baguette, 124

Balas ruby, 124

Bangle, **106**
defined, 124

Basse-taille, 124

Bat, miniature, in jewellery, 114

Beading tool, method used for making
metal spheres, 47

Benson, Messrs J. W., work of, 108, 109

Bezel, 124

Bijouterie, 125

Birds, imitations of, at Paris (1867), 31

Birmingham, growth of, in metal-work
industries, 16
leaders in sphere of popular jewellery, 38
manufacture of cut-steel jewellery in,
74, 75, 76, 80

*Birmingham and the Midland Hardware
District*, W. C. Aitken, 95

Bloodstone, 63

Bolsover, Thomas, discovery of fusion of
silver and copper, 19

Bort, 125

Bossing, technique, 97

Boulton, Matthew, factories producing
jewellery in 18th century, 16

Box setting, 125

Bracelets, **67, 83, 90, 100, 106**
by Castellani, 46
elaborate and heavy in 1860s and
1870s, 32

Brilliant cut, 125
Briolette, 125
Bristol stone, 125
Brogden, John, jeweller, 35, 48, 49, 113
Brooches, 18, 23, 24, 34, 46, 56, 62, 78, 83, 90, 99, 100, 121, 122
  by Giuliano, 46
  early Victorian, 34
  in High Victorian style, 34
  in 'Holbein' or 'Tudor' style, 61, 62
  in Neo-Classic style, 62
  insect, 115
Browning, Robert, quotations from, 10, 123
Bruting, 125
Bullion, 125
Burnishing, the process, 98

Cabochon, 125
  garnet brooch, 56, 90
Cairngorm, surrounded by pearls and garnets, 39
Cameo-cutter, materials for, 29
Carbuncles, 40
  bracelet set with, 106
  brooch set with, 46
  motif set with, 99
Castellani, Fortunato Pio, Italian jeweller, 20, 42, 43, 44, 47, 50
  bracelet by, 46
  mosaic work revived by, 85
Castellani Collection, purchased by British Government, 49
Cameos, 125
  fashionable in High Victorian period, 29
  imitation shell, 86
  Renaissance and classical, copied, 29
  shell, 85, 86, 105
  the true gemstone, 29
Carat, 125
Cat's eye, brief account of, 63
  in work of Castellani, 49
Cellini, Benvenuto, 116, 117
  Treatises, 47

Champlevé enamelling, 95, 96
  defined, 125
Chasing, 125
Chatelaine, 126
Chatoyancy, 126
Christofle, goldsmith, 52
Chrysoprase, in work of Castellani, 49
Claw-set, 126
Cleal, William, manufacturer of human hair jewellery, 92
Cleavage, 126
Cloisonné enamelling, 95, 96
  defined, 126
Collet set, 126
Colour, jewellery lavish with, 57
Cooper, E. R., ear-piercing illustration after, 68
Coral, brief account of, 63
  comment by Sala on, 91
  decline of, 26
  in early Victorian jewellery, 88
  suite in, 89
Cornelian, 63
Costume jewellery, the basis of, 66
Creole ear-ring, 126
Crescent, diamond, 39
Crown, 126
Culet, 126
Cut-steel jewellery, 73–5

Damascening, technique, 97
Deeley, W. G., comments on fashions at the Paris Exhibition (1867), 30
  report on work of Castellani, 48, 49
  report on work of Mr Brogden, 49
  report on work of Mr Phillips, 50
Derby, former centre of the popular jewellery trade, 75
Diamanté, 126
Diamonds, bouquet of, by Hunt and Roskell, 25
  bracelets set with, 62, 78
  brilliant cut, attributed to Vincenti Peruzzi, 14

briolette set with, **39**

brooches set with, **23, 24, 34, 46, 61, 99, 100**

discovery of the brilliant cut for, 13, 42

in jewellery at the Paris Exhibition of 1867, 30–2

in rising-sun motif, **39**

necklaces set with, **23, 24, 33, 90**

parures set with, 21

rings set with, **83**

rose cut, 13, 14

sprays set with, **23, 39, 40**

table cut, 14

tiara set with, **18**

use not to be entirely restricted to married women, 28

Die-stamping, prevalent in cheap jewellery, 98

Doublet, 126

Ear piercing, illustrated in print after E. R. Cooper, **68**

Ear-rings, 55, 67, 77, 78, **105**

after the marbles from Nineveh, 25

Creole, 36, 126

return to favour of, 36

Edinburgh, popular jewellery manufactured in, 75

Egyptian jewellery, 69, 98

Elba, work of jeweller on, 102

Electro-gilding, the process, 80

a 19th-century innovation, 98

Electro-plating, in cheap jewellery, 16

Elizabethan ornament, 35

Emerald cut, 126

Emeralds, brooches set with, **18, 24, 78**

ear-rings set with, **77**

necklace set with, **77**

Emmanuel, H., jeweller, 35

Enamelling, encrusted, 95, 96

Limoges, 95

the three mediaeval techniques, **95, 96**

Engraving, gemstone, technique, 29, 30

metal, defined, 129

Etruscan jewellery, 101

Etruscan style, 41–52, 80

Fabergé, Peter Carl, jeweller, 116–119

minuterie by the House of, **128**

Facet, 129

Faceted stone, Age of the, 13

Fede ring, 129

Ferronière, 129

Filigree work, 41–52

defined, 129

in brooches, **34, 62**

in turquoise and pearl suite, **67**

technique, 97

Fire, 129

Flint glass, 129

Florentine mosaic work, **46**

Flowers, imitation of, at Paris (1867), 31

motifs in diamond jewellery, 21

Flux, 129

Fobs and seals, 30

Foil, 129

Fontenay, Parisian jeweller, 47

French jet, easily detected, 91

French jewellery, design the principal feature of, 35

ornamentation, characteristic from its variety, 35

Froment-Meurice, French jeweller, 22, 52

Garnets, among favourite stones, 60

bracelet set with, **84**

brief account of, 63

brooches set with, **56, 90**

cairngorm surrounded by, **39**

pendant set with, **90**

Garrard, R. and S., and Co., jewellers, 59, 113

Gaskin, Arthur, necklace and brooch designed by, **121**

Gem-cutting, 71, 104, 107

Gilbert, Alfred, presidential badge and chain by, **112**

Gilt Toy Trade, 66

Gipsy setting, 129
Girandole, 129
Girdle, 129
Giuliano, Carlo, jeweller, 20, 48, 50, 119
  enamel brooch by, **46**
Glass-making industry, 16
Glyptic, 129
Gold, bloom on, technique, 50
  coloured, 50, 93, 94
  filigree, 41–52; *see also* Filigree work
  granulated; *see* Granulated goldwork
  in Victorian jewellery, 93, 94
  pseudo, Mr Pinchbeck's formula for, 19
  quality of, 93
Goldsmiths Hall, Wardens of, 19
Gothic revival, 22, 25
Grain, weight, 129
Granaglia, antique method of making, 47
  see also Granulated goldwork
Granulated goldwork, 41, 43, 44, **46**,
  47, 48, 50, 51, **56**, **67**
  defined, 130
  the process, 98, 101, 102
Graver, 130
Great Exhibition, 1851, *Morning
  Chronicle* leader-writer on, 53
  'naturalistic' representation at, 22, 25
  typical display at, 25
Great Exhibition, 1851, Official Catalogue,
  Scottish jewellery recorded in, 87
Greek style, 30, 31, 35
Greenbury, Isaac, jet jewellery by, 91
Grisaille, 130

Hair jewellery, 92, 114
Hancock and Sons, jewellers, 31, 35
Hardman, of Birmingham, jewellery by,
  111
Herculaneum, excavations and discoveries
  at, 20, 41, 57
'Holbein' style, brooch in, **61**
Hunt and Roskell, jewellers, 35, 52
  pieces at the Great Exhibition by, 25

Identification of Victorian jewellery from
  classic originals, 50
Illusion setting, 130
Indian influence, 36
Insect brooches, 115
Intaglio work, 29, 30
  defined, 130
In the round, 130

Jackson, Holbrook, writing on Arts and
  Crafts Movement, 113
Jacquin, French jeweller, 82
Jade, 63
Jasper, 63
Jet, in popular jewellery, 91
Jewellery, detachable, popularity for
  formal wear in the 1860s, 30
  English and French compared, 32, 35
  Georgian, dominated by French
    fashions, 14
  mass production of, 66
  popular, its ancestry and development
    in the 19th century, 66–92
  semi-precious, of the 19th century,
    53–65
*Jewellery and Gilt Toy Trade, Report
  on the*, James Pamplin, 35
Jewellery Manufacture (1887),
  Birmingham, 38
Joaillerie, 130

Lacombe, *Tableau de Londres* (1777), **15**
Lamerie, Paul de, silversmith, 14
Lap, 130
Lapis lazuli, brief account of, 63
  in work of Castellani, 49
Layard, Sir Austen Henry, *Nineveh and
  its Remains*, 26
London, manufacture of popular
  jewellery in, 75
Loudon, *Encyclopaedia of Cottage, Villa
  and Farm Architecture* (1833), 22

Lunate, 130
Lustre, 130

Marcasite, 73
  defined, 130
Marquise, 104, 130
Mass-produced jewellery, foundations of,
  16
Materials, techniques and, 93–107
Metal-work industries, growth of Bir-
  mingham into headquarters of, 16
Millegrain setting, 51
  defined, 130
Minuterie, 130
Mixed cut, 131
Mohs's scale, 131
Moorish style, 27
Morris, William, quoted, 110
Mosaic work, fashionable in Early
  Victorian jewellery, 85
  floral design on brooch in, **46**
  imitation, 42
Motif, Assyrian, introduced into English
  jewellery, 26
  rising-sun, 39
Mourning jewellery, 19
Muller, Bertha, portrait of Queen
  Victoria by, **127**

'Naturalistic' Movement, 22, 25
Navette, 104, 130
Necklaces, 24, 33, 55, 56, 61, 77, 78,
  84, 90, 105, 121
  in Greek style, 30
  rivière, amethyst the ideal stone for, 58
Neo-Classicism, 42, 57, **62**
Niello, defined, 131
  technique, 96, 97
Nineveh and its Remains, Sir Austen
  Henry Layard, 26

Olivine, 64
Onyx, brief account of, 64
  in work of Castellani, 49

Opals, brief account of, 64
  brooch set with, **34**
  discovery of mines in Australia, 57
  necklace set with, **90**
  widely used, 59
Oriental influence, 36

Paillons, 131
Pamplin, James, jeweller, quoted, 35, 82
Paravagua and Casella, jewellers, 88
Paris, dictator of Europe's fashions,
  15, 16
Paris Exhibition, 1867, 50
  committee sent to, 48
*Paris Exhibition of 1867, Notes and
  Sketches of the*, George Augustus Sala,
  43
Parure, defined, 131
  18th-century fashion revived, 19, 21
Paste, composition of, 69, 70
  defined, 131
  in mediaeval jewellery, 70
  long history of, 69
Pavé setting, 39, 131
Pavilion, section of gemstone, 131
Peacock, baroque pearl in form of, **122**
Pearls, bangle set with, **106**
  baroque, defined, 124
  blister, 125
  brooches set with, **46, 61, 62, 67, 78,
    99, 100**
  cairngorm surrounded by, 39
  ear-rings set with, **67, 77**
  freshwater, 51, 88
  imitation, 82
  in form of peacock, **122**
  most fashionable ornament for a young
    girl, 28
  necklace set with, **77**
  ring set with, **61**
  seed-, 131
  suite set with, **67**
  tiara set with, **18**

Pendant, star, **84**
Pendeloque, 131
Peridots, 58
  brief account of, 64
  ear-rings set with, **78**
  necklace set with, **78**
Peruzzi, Vincenti, the brilliant cut
    attributed to, 14
Phillips, Robert, jeweller, 44, 48, 49,
    50, 52, 113, 119
Pinchbeck, 19, 80
  defined, 131
Plated jewellery, 81
Platinum, as setting for diamonds, 108,
    115
  first discovery of, 94
  scarcity of, 93–95
Plique-à-jour, enamelling, 131
Pocock, Alfred, modeller and carver, 118
Pompeii, influence of discoveries at, 20,
    41, 57
Pugin, A. W. N., 22
  jewellery designed by, **111**

Queen, The (1899), notice from, 108,
    109

Ramsden, Omar, jeweller, 113
Ravenscroft, discoveries of, 72
Red cornelian, in work of Castellani, 49
Renaissance work, imitation of, 51
Repoussé, defined, 131
  technique, 97, 98, **99**
Rhinestone, 60
  defined, 131
Rings, 30, **61**, **83**, **99**
Rivière, 58, 94
  defined, 131
Rock-crystal, often used by Victorian
    jeweller, 60
Rolled-gold jewellery, high standard of,
    81
Roman ornament, 35

Romantic Movement, influence of, 21,
    22, 31
Rose cut, 131
Rouge, jewellers', 130
Rouvenat, M., French jeweller, 35
Rubies, brooches set with, **18**, **24**, **34**,
    61, **78**, **100**
  ear-rings, set with, **77**
  necklace set with, **77**
  spray set with, **39**

St Angelo de Vado, craftsmen from, 43
Sala, George Augustus, quoted, 35, 43,
    52, 91
Sapphires, necklace and ear-rings set
    with, 24
  ring set with, **61**
Sard, 64
Sardonyx, 64
Saw-piercing, technique, 97
Schliemann, Dr, discoveries by, in
    Greece and Asia Minor, 36
Scott, Sir Walter, influence of, 86
  reference to an ill-omened opal by, 59
Scottish jewellery, vogue for, 86–8
Settings, types of, 103, 104
  becoming lighter by 1887, 37
Sévigné, 19, 116
  defined, 131
Shakespeare, enamelled portrait by
    W. Essex of, 25
Shank, 132
Sheffield plate, invention of, 19
Silver, 93, 94
Silver industry, growth of Birmingham
    into headquarters of the, 16
Smallwork, 118, 130
  defined, 132
Society of Arts, committee sent to Paris
    Exhibition by, 48
Spinel, 58
  brief account of, 64
Sprays, 23, **39**, **40**
Stabler, Harold, 113

Stick pins, 83
Stomacher, 116
Strass, defined, 132
Strass, Josef, discoveries of, 72
  paste formula of, 70
Suite, defined, 132
  turquoise and pearl, 67
Synthetic stones, 132

Table, facet, 132
Techniques and materials, 93–107
Theophilus, mediaeval monk-jeweller, 47
Tiara, gold, set with diamonds and
    pearls, 18
Topaz, 29
  bracelet set with, 100, 106
  brief account of, 64
Tortoises, real, bejewelled, 114, 115
Tourmaline, 64
Traquair, Phoebe, jeweller, 113
Treatises, Cellini, 47
Troy, excavations at, 36, 57
'Tudor' style, brooch in, 61
Turkish style, 27
Turquoise, bracelet set with, 83
  brief account of, 64
  brooch set with, 18
  motif, 99
  rings set with, 61, 83
  suite set with, 67

Tutankhamen, ornaments found in
    tomb of, 98

Victoria, Queen, portrait by Lady
    Abercrombie, 45
  enamelled portrait by J. Haslem, 25
  portrait by Bertha Muller, 127
Victorian, Early, styles, 21 *et seq.*
  High, styles, 28–38

Walpole, Horace, comment on Sheffield,
    19
Watches, jewellery made from, 115
Watchmaker, Jeweller, and Silversmith,
    quoted, 28, 114
Wheat motifs, 21
Whitby jet industry, rise of, 91
Wilson, Henry, jeweller, 113
Winterhalter, F., enamelled portrait of
    Queen Victoria after, 25
Wire, use of fine-drawn gold and silver
    by Indian jewellers, 51
Wright, J. S., writing on effects of the
    machine, 102, 103
Wyatt, Sir Matthew Digby, *Journal of
    Design*, 26

Zircon, 64